A Celebration of Decorative Painting

"Plums" by Bette Byrd

Roses by Bette Byrd
See pages 10 & 11 for instructions

A Celebration of Decorative Painting

Plaid's 25th Anniversary Book

TWENTY-FIVE YEARS

PLAID®

SILVER ANNIVERSARY

PLAID ENTERPRISES, INC.

Editor: Mickey Baskett
Editorial Assistant: Susan Mickey
Photo Styling: Susan Mickey, Laney McClure, Lenos Key, Kirsten Jones
Photography: Jerry Mucklow, Jeff Herr, Jimmy George
Copy: Sylvia Carroll, Phyllis Mueller
Graphics: Karen Turpin

Library of Congress Cataloging-in-Publication Data Available

Published by Plaid Enterprises, Inc.
3225 Westech Drive, Norcross, GA 30092
www.plaidonline.com
800-842-4197

©2001 by Plaid Enterprises, Inc.

Printed in the USA
All rights reserved.

ISBN #1-55895-000-1

TITLE PAGE CALLIGRAPHY BY KEN BROWN

Ken Brown created the lovely calligraphy for the title pages of this book. Ken is a master calligrapher and has created a technique for sharing his intriguing yet simple technique. Since 1972 Ken Brown has been teaching this extraordinary method of calligraphy through his company, The Ken Brown Studio of Calligraphic Art. Introduced to the art of lettering in a college architecture class, Ken became so enamored with the art of lettering that he left his training to do nothing else but calligraphy. After many years of working at various jobs, Ken was finally able to make calligraphy his full time career. Tens of millions of impressions of his calligraphy have appeared on Public Television programs, art prints, magazine ads, videos, kits, books, calligraphy markers, and various other tools.

In his two books, *Brush Lettering with Ken Brown #9459* and *Calligraphy with Ken Brown® – Marker Handbook #9578* published by Plaid, Ken presents his fool-proof method of making beautiful letters and numbers with brushes or with calligraphy markers that Ken has designed

Dedication

Bette Byrd had a painting career that spanned several decades. She was loved by many and she influenced and taught multitudes. For many years she taught oil painting and owned a painting shop where her gift for teaching and painting projected her into a full blown career of teaching and consulting. When acrylic paints were introduced, Bette was one of the first artists to embrace acrylics for decorative painting. She helped Plaid Enterprises develop their line of FolkArt® paints as well as helped to educate painters about the attributes of that paint. Plaid greatly relied on Bette's expertise and counsel when developing new colors, new products, and new book authors and artists.

When Plaid needed a line of decorative painting brushes to pair with their high quality paints, they called upon Bette to design these brushes for them. Later, Bette became the owner of this brush line and started her company, **Bette Byrd Brushes.** Today these excellent brushes are still available for the painter to enjoy.

Bette was quite active in The Society of Decorative Painters, serving as the president of that organization for a term. Bette was always outspoken about the importance of the painting industry. Her influence was widespread and she will be missed by many.

The photo at left is a project from Bette's last book, Furniture in Bloom. *Bette finished this book shortly before her death on January 11, 2001. This book was printed in May 2001. The two photos at the bottom of this page are Rosemaling projects Bette painted in the early 1980's.*

Table of Contents

Page 15

Page 19

Page 23

Page 27

Page 31

Page 35

Page 39

Page 45

A Celebration of Decorative Painting

25th Anniversary Edition

Presenting 25 Projects to Celebrate 25 Years of Painting

Painting brings joy and beauty, and it knows no time restraints. Beauty is eternal. The designs presented in this book seem as fresh and beautiful as they did when they were published years ago. You will find 25 project designs – many from as long ago as 20 years – many are just a few years old. Many of the painters whose work you will see in this book have made a career of painting and teaching for 25 years or more. Others, honored here, are new to the art, but have learned much from those paving the way for them.

I don't like to admit it, but I have been editing Plaid's instruction books for 25 years. I have seen many wonderful painters dedicate their time and life to teaching others the joy of painting.

Beautiful roses in a basket painted by Gloria Koskey

Fun painting projects from Susan Fouts-Kline

Trudy Beard's first book with Plaid

When I started digging through the archives to find photos or instructions to use in this Celebration book, I found myself daydreaming and getting teary-eyed about all the wonderful artists I have had the pleasure to work with. I have learned much, as I know their students did.

In trying to pick 25 designs to be included in this book, I decided to choose designs that were painted with acrylics using decorative painting strokework techniques, and use materials that are available today. Projects in some older books used oil paints and/or materials that are not available. It was very hard to pick just 25 painters because there have been so many painters that have been important to Plaid. I am reminded of *Gloria Koskey* and her beautiful oil-painting style that looks aged; and *Brenda Jansen* who painted the most glorious flowers on taffeta. There are others who are new to Plaid and have published their first books such as Trudy Beard, Linda Biggs, Susan Embry, Susan Fouts-Kline, and Bob Pennycook. Each author brings beauty to our world.

Mickey Baskett

A watercolor technique by Linda Biggs

No one could paint on fabric like Brenda Jansen

Gorgeous still life paintings from **Rustic Still Lifes** *by Canadian artist Bob Pennycook*

Ingenious techniques by Carol Mays

Roses

By Bette Byrd

See photo on page 2

1 Gather These Supplies

FolkArt® Acrylic Colors:
Burgundy #957
Wrought Iron #925
Rose Garden #754
Aspen Green #646
Spring Rose #767
Bayberry #922
Buttercream #614
Wicker White #901
Licorice #938

Bette Byrd Brushes:
1/4" & 1/2" Angular
#6 & #8 Shaders
Fine Liner or #00 Scroller

Other Supplies:
FolkArt® Extender
FolkArt® Waterbase Varnish
12" round wooden frame
9" circle of 1/8" birch wood to fit frame opening
Gold Leafing Kit

2 Preparation

1. Gold leaf the wooden frame using the Gold Leafing Kit.
2. Paint the circle of birch wood with several coats of Licorice, sanding between coats.

3 Paint the Design

Hints for Painting Roses:
1. Use angular brush with the darkest paint value on heel (short side of the angle) and lightest value on the tip (longest side of the angle).
2. Keep three (3) paint values on your brush for subtle contrast.
3. Work from the back edge of the rose and come forward.
4. Petals should be very close together and staggered.
5. Relax!

Rose:
Use the Angular Brush:
1. Fill in center of rose with Burgundy + Rose Garden.
2. Apply these colors in a "C" shape at bottom of rose.
3. Load "dirty" brush with Buttercream + Wicker White on tip of angular brush and paint individual back petals, starting at the upper back of the rose and working forward. Keep the most pressure on the heel of your brush.
4. Paint inside rows of front petals with lightest value on outside edges using Rose Garden + Spring Rose + Wicker White. Pick up a touch of Buttercream with the White on some petals.
5. The most outside petals are made with a light value + Wicker White. Remember to pull some of these outside petals onto body of rose.
6. Shade or highlight individual petals, if necessary. Remember the more open front petals are the lightest value.

Rosebud:
Paint the bud petals using the darker rose colors with a touch of Spring Rose + Wicker White on the outside petal edges.

Leaves and Calyx:
1. Load shader brush with Aspen Green and side load with Bayberry. Base coat leaves, keeping darker value in center of leaf and lighter value toward outside.
2. Shade leaves and calyx with Aspen Green + Wrought Iron and Wrought Iron. Keep darkest value at base and down vein line.
3. Highlight outside edges with Bayberry + White.
4. Add a touch of Burgundy and/or Rose Garden to some leaves for contrast, especially at the base and near the center vein line. Blend well.
5. The small leaf near the bud is the lightest value leaf.
6. Add veins curving them slightly to the outside edge of the leaf.
7. Paint stems Aspen Green with a touch of Bayberry as highlight.
8. Paint squiggles using the scroller brush loaded with very thin Aspen Green + Bayberry.

4 Finish

1. Allow painting and frame to dry thoroughly.
2. Finish with varnish. ❏

Pattern – Actual Size

Supplies For Decorative Painting

🦢 FolkArt® Paints

FolkArt® Acrylic Colors are high quality bottle acrylic paints. Their rich and creamy formulation and long open time make them perfect for decorative painting. They are offered in a huge range of wonderful, pre-mixed colors and in gleaming metallic shades. Cleanup is easy with soap and water.

FolkArt® Artists' Pigments™ are pure colors that are perfect for mixing your own shades. Their intense colors and creamy consistency are wonderful for blending, shading, and highlighting.

FolkArt® Metallic Colors are paints that add subtle iridescence or a metallic sheen.
Because FolkArt® paints are acrylic-based, cleanup is easy with soap and water.

🦢 FolkArt® Painting Mediums

FolkArt® Blending Gel Medium #867 is a truly revolutionary product that makes acrylics feel more like oil paints. If you place a sufficient amount of Blending Gel on the surface to be decorated then place the FolkArt® Artists' Pigments on top with a good deal of color application you can blend your colors wet into wet. The critical aspect to achieving the oil-blended look is the volume of gel and paint on the surface and keeping your brush out of the water.

FolkArt® Floating Medium #868 is specially formulated for mixing with any of the FolkArt paints to create a thinned consistency that will "float" over the surface. It will not dilute the pigmentation.

FolkArt® Glazing Medium #693 can turn any FolkArt® paint into a transparent colored glaze to create faux and paint finishes on your accessory pieces. Mix acrylic paint into the Glazing Medium slowly to create a transparent mixture. Glazing Medium is a great way for a decorative painter who is unfamiliar with faux finishes to experiment.

FolkArt® Extender #947 increases drying time and transparency of the paint for glazing, antiquing, or washing.

FolkArt® Crackle Medium #694 gives weathered, time-worn finish to projects.

🦢 Brushes

Many artists have their own preference for brands of brushes. The most important thing is that you purchase the highest quality brushes you can afford. When painting an area use the largest brush that will fit to accommodate an area. Choose a variety of flats, rounds, and liners.

🦢 Finishes

FolkArt® ClearCote™ Matte Acrylic Sealer #789: Spray with this product after your basecoat has dried and before you begin the painting processes. This will help keep the surface clean of smudges. Also mist the surface with this sealer after the painting is dry and before you varnish.

FolkArt® Artist's Varnish: A protective coating is essential over your decorative painting on wood. FolkArt® Artist's Varnish dries clear and is non-yellowing. It's available in matte, satin, and gloss sheens in 2 oz., 4 oz., and 8 oz. sizes.

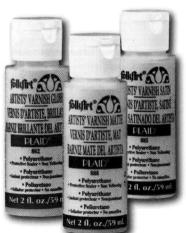

Supplies For Decorative Painting

❧ Miscellaneous Supplies

Brush Basin®, for rinsing brushes
White and gray transfer paper and **stylus**, for transferring designs
Palette knife, for mixing paints
Paper towels, for blotting
Ruler, for measuring
Pencils, for marking
Spray mister bottle with water

❧ Surface Preparation

Wood:
1. Fill any holes or flaws in the wood with wood filler (available at any building center or hardware store). Allow the filler to dry thoroughly.
2. Sand with a grit of paper that will remove any rough surface. Use a finer grit to finish. Develop the habit of sanding in the direction of the grain of the wood.
3. Remove any wood dust with your damp cloth.
4. Seal your wood. Dilute matte finish FolkArt® Artist Varnish with clean water for this step.
5. Let dry. Sand your piece again with 320-grit paper or finer.

Porcelain Bisque:
Wash thoroughly with soap and warm water. Rinse well and dry. No other preparation is needed.

Terra Cotta Flower Pots:
1. Sand the pieces with a fine grit of sandpaper.
2. Wash thoroughly with warm soap and water. Rinse well.
3. Place in your oven at about 250 degrees for several hours to evaporate any moisture.
4. Seal only the outside if you intend to use it for plants. Seal the inside as well, if you are using it for other purposes, or lining with another pot.

Papier Mache:
1. Seal with one coat of all purpose sealer. The moisture in the sealer may raise bubbles on the paper surface. These almost always go flat when the sealer and paper dry.
2. Basecoat with the color of your choice.

Metal:
Preprimed metal surfaces require no preparation...just start painting. If the metal is not pre-primed, wash with a vinegar water solution, spray with sealer, then add two coats of basepaint.

❧ Finishing your projects

After you've finished painting, you'll need to protect your project with several layers of FolkArt Artists' Varnish. This is a durable, polyurethane varnish. Two coats is fine but five or six light coats are better. Obviously the more, the better the protection. If you're using a number of coats and you prefer a matte finish, start with gloss varnish then use the matte varnish for your final two coats. Matte has fillers in it which could cloud your painting if you're using many layers (like when your varnishing a floorcloth).

If you have applied two coats of varnish, then there is no need for sanding. Sand only after you have about three or four layers on the surface. Then wet sand with 400 grit wet and dry sandpaper. Remove the sludge with a wet paper towel and repeat sanding with 600 grit sandpaper. Then, after cleaning off the sludge, repeat with a further two or three coats of varnish. You could also wax the final finish, using a good furniture paste wax.

Nothing protects your paint job against the sun. No matter what product you use to protect your painting, if you leave the project in direct sunlight constantly, the colors will fade. ❏

Sunflower Pot

by Sue Bailey

Paint a flowerpot and invite your friends for dessert. Or you can use this pot for planting or gift giving. Try the recipe for Dirt Cake to fill this beautiful pot for your home or patio. This design first appeared in Sue's book **Pots with a Purpose** *published by Plaid Enterprises, Inc. in 1995.*

Sue has been painting for over 25 years. She has authored numerous painting books including *Fancy Pants* and *Pots with a Purpose*. Starting her painting career in oils, Sue learned to love acrylics because she could paint with them on hard surfaces as well as on fabric. Many of you will know Sue for her wonderful painted vests.

Sue is a master at painting fine art as well as decorative craft pieces. She is currently working on Portraits of her seven grandchildren; and is to be congratulated for finishing three paintings. With her busy teaching and traveling schedule, she still manages to finish one Portrait each year.

Sue's husband John is supportive of what she does and travels with her to help with the shows she attends. Her three sons and daughters-in-law also support her in her work.

You may contact this artist at:
Sue Bailey
2150 McDuffie Road
Austell, Georgia 30106
Or call: 770-941-5571
E-mail: suebpub@bellsouth.net
website: http:/personal.atl.bellsouth.net/atl/suebpub

Recipe for Dirt Cake

Crush **1 Large package Oreo Cookies** (a food processor is great for this). Set Aside.
Combine **2 packages French Vanilla Instant Pudding Mix** with **3-1/2 Cups Milk**.
Stir until pudding begins to thicken. Add **1 small carton Cool Whip**. Mix. Set aside.

Cream together **1/4 Cup butter**, **8 oz. Cream Cheese**, and **1 Cup Confectioner's Sugar**.
Combine cream cheese mixture with pudding mixture.

Place a layer of cookies in a plastic pot liner. Add a layer of pudding-cream cheese mixture. Alternate layers ending with a cookie layer. ❑

Inside this lovely flower pot is a "Dirt Cake."
Serving this yummy cake in a flower pot only adds
to its charm. It is perfect for summer entertaining
on the patio. I found a plastic liner bowl that
would just fit inside the flower pot. I filled the
bottom part of the pot with floral foam so the liner
would come to the top of the pot. Use the trowel to
serve your "dirt cake."

Sunflower Pot

By Sue Bailey

1 Gather These Supplies

Folk Art ® Acrylic Colors:
Hunter Green #406

FolkArt® Artists' Pigments:
Pure Black #479
Titanium White #480
Burnt Sienna #943
Burnt Umber #462
Medium Yellow #455

Painting Surface
Clay Pot, 10"
Trowel with Wooden Handle

Other Supplies
FolkArt® Waterbase Varnish
Fine Sandpaper
Tack Cloth
Plastic Liner for pot, 10"
Stencil Blank Material
Scotch Brand Magic Tape, 1" wide
Craft Knife
Small Artificial Sunflower
Glue E-6000

2 Preparation

1. Base rim of pot and handle of trowel with Pure Black. Base lower part of pot with Titanium White. Let dry thoroughly.
2. Trace pattern for checked design on rim onto stencil blank material. Cut out with craft knife. Position stencil on rim of pot. Stencil checks with 2 coats of Titanium White Let dry thoroughly. **Note:** You could also transfer the checks pattern or outline them with 1" tape, and then paint with 2 coats Titanium White.
3. To Create vertical stripes on lower part of pot, position 1" wide strips of tape 1-1/2" apart. Paint between strips with Pure Black. Second coat if needed. Let dry thoroughly. Carefully remove tape.
4. Trace and transfer to pot.

3 Paint the Design

Petals:
1. Paint Sunflower petals with a light cover of Burnt Sienna.
2. Overstroke with Medium Yellow and Medium Yellow + Titanium White. Shade at bases and to separate with Burnt Sienna.

Centers:
1. Paint Centers with Burnt Umber. Dab on Burnt Sienna, Medium Yellow, and Titanium White.
2. Add dots around centers with Pure Black.

Leaves:
1. Paint Leaves with Hunter Green.
2. Shade leaves with Hunter Green + Pure Black, starting at the outer edges of the leaves and pulling in, leaving the background color showing in the center. Shade between the leaves, adding more Pure Black if needed.
3. Highlight with Medium Yellow and Medium Yellow + Titanium White.
4. Using a liner brush, paint veins in leaves with Medium Yellow + Titanium White.

Trowel Handle:
1. Sand the handle of the towel with a fine sandpaper.
2. Wipe the handle of the trowel with a tack cloth removing sanding dust.
3. Apply tape to handle to create 1" checked design. Paint with Titanium White #480. Let dry thoroughly. Carefully remove tape.

4 Finish

1. When painting is complete and paint is thoroughly dry, apply Folk Art Waterbase Varnish for a satin finish, Folk Art Clear Cote Hi Shine Glaze for a deep gloss finish, or Folk Art Clear Cote Extra-Thick Glaze for a shiny finish. Let Dry.
2. Glue artificial sunflower to handle of trowel.
3. Assemble Dirt Cake in plastic liner. Place plastic liner in pot. Decorate with additional cookies, if desired. ❏

Enlarge 200% for actual size

16

Sunflowers

1. Basecoat all petals with Burnt Sienna. Overstroke with Yellow Medium. Paint centers with Burnt Umber. Paint leaves and stems with Hunter Green.

2. Highlight petals with Yellow Medium + Titanium White. Let some of the Burnt Sienna show through.
3. With scruffy brush, dab Burnt Sienna and Yellow Medium in flower centers.
4. Highlight leaves and stems with Yellow Medium + Titanium White.
5. Add vein lines with Titanium White.

$\mathscr{F}$eatherbed $\mathscr{I}$nn

by $\mathscr{A}$urelia Conway

*This whimsical painted Gourd is from **Gourds ... Naturally Sensational**. The painted gourd can be used as a decorative gourd or a birdhouse for feathered friends.*

$\mathscr{A}$urelia has been painting for 32 years and teaching for twelve years. She lives on a farm called "Hummingbird Hill" with her husband, Jim, in southern Indiana. She has been a member of the *Society of Decorative Painters* (SDP) for twelve years and a member of the INDY Decorative Artists chapter for three years. She has taught at the NSTDP National Convention, Extrav, Mini Conventions, Chapter Seminars, and locally in the *ArtColumbus Studio/Gallery* and exhibits at most of the national shows and conventions.

Aurelia has two grown children and many friends who have been supportive of her artistic endeavors.

You may contact this artist at:
Aurelia Conway
Hummingbird Hill at 10285 S. 500 E
Elizabethtown, IN 47232
Phone: 812-579-6510
Email: aconway@hsonline.net.
You can see more of her work by visiting her website at **http://www.tolenet.com.hummingbird_hill.**

Barn Siding Painting Worksheet

Step 1: Using a flat Shader, paint boards in a single stroke.

Step 2: Shade top of boards.

Step 3: Highlight base of boards.

Feather Bed Inn

By Aurelia Conway

1 Gather These Supplies

FolkArt® Acrylic Colors:
Basil Green #645
Pastel Green #466
Dove Grey #708
French Vanilla #431
Icy White #701
Licorice #938
Midnight #964
Hunter Green #406

FolkArt® Artists' Pigments:
Brilliant Ultramarine #484
Burnt Sienna #943
Payne's Gray #477
Raw Sienna #452
Raw Umber #485
Sap Green #458
Titanium White #480
True Burgundy #456
Warm White #649
Yellow Ochre #917

Painting Surface:
Martin or kettle gourd, approx. 9" x 12-1/2"

Other Supplies:
Shader Brushes #4,#6,#10
Angular Brushes size 1/2
Liner Brush #1 short
Round Brush #2,#6
Deerfoot sizes1/4" and 3/8"
Decorator Products™ Ocean Sponge #31050
Black permanent pen
FolkArt® Outdoor Sealer, matte finish #864

2 Preparation

1. Basecoat entire gourd with French Vanilla. Let dry.
2. Transfer pattern to gourd; omit fine details.
3. If using as a birdhouse, cut hole for bird entrance.

3 Paint the Design

Roofs:
1. Basecoat both roofs and dormer with Dove Grey.
2. Basecoat roof trim with Hunter Green, using a #4 flat brush. Shade along top of trim with Raw Umber.
3. Along each roof, float a series of staggered half moon shapes with Icy White. Shade under each with Payne's Gray.
4. Shade the top of each roof, under the trim, and along the edge of the dormer on right side with Raw Umber.

Dormer:
1. Paint dormer trim with Hunter Green. Shade along top edge of left side with Raw Umber.
2. Basecoat the triangular inner area with Yellow Ochre.
3. Paint the semi-circle at center bottom with True Burgundy.
4. Shade to create the sunburst detailing with Raw Umber.

Windows:
1. Basecoat inside of windows with diluted Payne's Gray.
2. Float curtains with Warm White. Add Warm White detailing with a toothpick.
3. Paint inner window trim with Titanium White #480. Shade with Licorice under the grills, but keep it light.
4. Paint outer window trim with Hunter Green, using a #2 flat brush.
5. Add a small True Burgundy block in each corner.
6. Shade bottom and right side on outside of each window with Raw Umber.

Siding Boards:
Refer to Siding Technique Painting Worksheet, using colors given below.
1. Draw board lines, aligning them with the windows.
2. Float along board lines with Yellow Ochre.
3. Shade board areas with Raw Umber where siding meets roof.

Door:
1. Basecoat with True Burgundy.
2. Paint door inner trim with Titanium White and outer trim with Hunter Green.
3. Shade around inside and outside edges of door with Raw Umber.
4. If painting bird hole instead of cutting it out, basecoat it with Licorice. Let dry. Highlight on right side with Payne's Gray and shade highlighted area on right side with Licorice.

Porch:
1. Basecoat porch posts with Hunter Green, using a #6 flat brush.
2. Paint stripes on posts with French Vanilla (top and bottom stripes) and True Burgundy (middle stripes).
3. Shade right side of posts with Raw Umber. Highlight left side of posts with Pastel Green.
4. Transfer placement of porch railings and upper ornamentation.
5. Shade back of porch and under door with Raw Umber.
6. Paint rails with Hunter Green. Paint spindles with Yellow Ochre + a touch of Titanium White.
7. Shade on right side of each spindle and under railing on each spindle with Raw Umber.
8. Paint front trim of porch with Hunter Green.
9. Paint lower kickplate with Raw Sienna.
10. Basecoat steps with Raw Sienna, then shade with Raw Umber.
11. Paint railing on steps the same as railing on porch, but add True Burgundy balls.

Bottom of Gourd/Foliage in Front of Inn:
Refer to Foliage Technique Painting Worksheet.
1. Sponge bottom up to the base of the inn with Raw Umber, then with Burnt Sienna.
2. Sponge area right next to foundation of inn with Sap Green, then highlight by sponging with Basil Green. This creates a garden area around the perimeter.
3. Basecoat the sign with two coats of Titanium White. Let dry.
4. Basecoat posts of sign with Raw Umber. Highlight with French Vanilla.
5. Write lettering with the permanent pen, when completely dry.
6. Stipple some foliage in the foreground with Sap Green. Highlight with stippled Basil Green. Stipple some of this foliage in front of the sign to set it back.
7. Using a small stippler brush, add flowers to the area in front of inn by double loading Titanium White with each of the following colors: Brilliant Ultramarine, True Burgundy, and Yellow Ochre. Don't overdo the flowers.
8. Shade around the base of all the foliage and at the bottom of the steps with Raw Umber.

4 Finish

When dry, seal with Outdoor Sealer. ❑

Pattern – Enlarge as needed to fit your gourd.

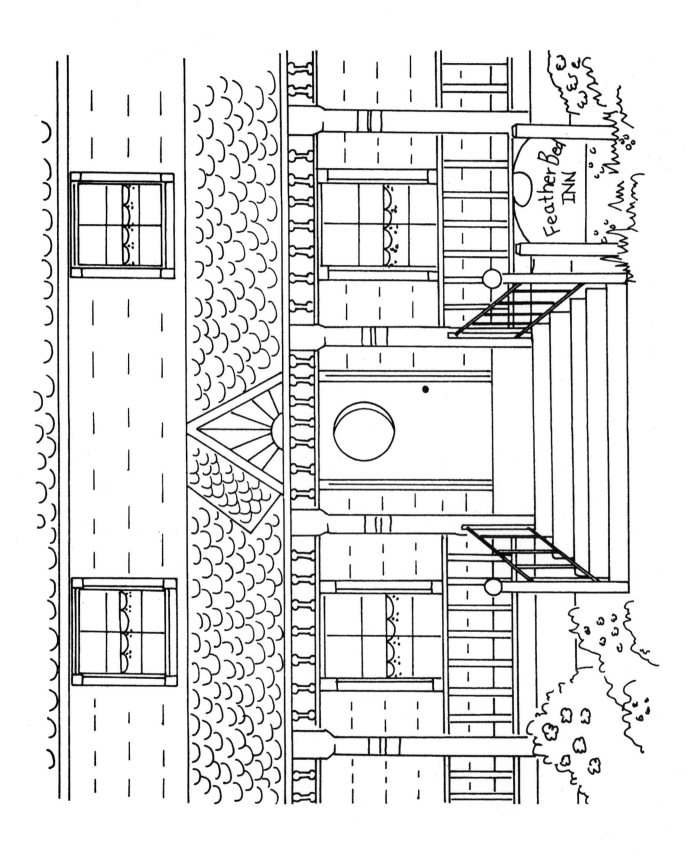

Friends Sign

painted by *Bess Daniel*

*This sign is an expression of Bess talent and creativity. It appeared in **Signs and Sayings** by Plaid Enterprises Inc. in 1994.*

B ess took her first painting class in an Adult Education course in Springfield, MA in 1974. It opened up a whole new world of enjoyment and challenges. Her first book for Plaid Enterprises, Inc. was *Christmas Keepsakes*. She has her CDA with the National Society of Decorative Painters and has had articles published in several magazines (including the "Angels Book, Vol. II" published by NSDP.)

This is the cover for one of the best selling books for Plaid and Bess. It was published in 1991.

22

Love suffereth long and is kind; Love beareth all things~believeth all things~hopeth all things~Endureth all things ~ Love never faileth ~ I Corinthians 13

Friends

Friends Plaque

∞

By Bess Daniel

1 Gather These Supplies

FolkArt® Acrylic Colors:
Heartland Blue #608
Barnyard Red #611
Taffy #902
English Mustard #959
Dark Brown #416
Nutmeg #944
Linen #420

FolkArt® Artists' Pigments:
Napthol Crimson #435
Raw Umber #485
Pure Black #479
Burnt Umber #462
Payne's Gray #477
Burnt Carmine #686
Warm White #649
Pure Orange #628

Painting Surface
Wooden Plaque or Frame approximately
6" high by 8" wide

Other Supplies:
Tube Oil Paint: Burnt Umber
3/4" wide Scotch Brand Magic Tape
FolkArt® Crackle Medium
FolkArt® Water Base Varnish

2 Preparation

1. Sand and seal the wood piece if necessary (many wooden frames come already sanded and sealed).
2. Basecoat inside the framed area with one coat of Taffy and the edges of the frame with three coats of Taffy. Let dry.
3. Apply 3/4" tape along the inner edge of the frame on all four sides (where the small lettering is placed). I used a craft knife to cut the edges and corners so they would be straight. Apply a fairly heavy coat of Crackle Medium to the outer edge of the frame (outside the taped area).
4. When the Crackle Medium is dry (about 2 hours) basecoat with one coat of Heartland Blue, starting at the frame is covered. Let dry.
5. Transfer the pattern inside the frame. Leave the tape in place while you paint the design.

3 Paint The Design

Basecoating
1. Basecoat the Bunny with Linen.
2. Basecoat the bear with "washy" Dark Brown (this will look red but don't worry).
3. Basecoat the bow on the bunny's head with Heartland Blue.
4. Basecoat the bow on the bear with Barnyard Red.
5. Basecoat the carrot with Pure Orange.

Bunny
1. Apply the first shading on the bunny softly with Nutmeg. Add the second shading with Raw Umber.
2. Place the highlights on the bunny with Taffy. Highlight the cheeks a little more with Warm White.
3. Add the fabric pattern under the ear with Heartland Blue using a liner brush.
4. Shade the carrot with Burnt Umber. Highlight with more Pure Orange and some Napthol Crimson.
5. Add the rope greens on the carrot with various browns from your palette.
6. Paint the short lines on the bunny with Burnt Umber to resemble stitching lines.
7. Paint the eye with Pure Black. Add a Warm White highlight.
8. Paint the lines and darker shading on the bow with Payne's Gray.

Bear:
1. Begin by floating some Raw Umber in the dark shaded areas. This is to help you with placement when you begin to stipple. Also add some Burnt Umber shading using a large brush and floated color.
2. Using a small mini-mop brush, stipple the bear in the dark areas with Burnt Umber and Raw Umber with light touches of Pure Black. Work to the lighter areas with Nutmeg followed by English Mustard.
3. Place the final highlights on the bear with Pure Orange + Warm White (add enough Pure Orange to keep this a peach color). Keep stippling with all of the colors mentioned above until he looks fluffy and furry.

4. Paint the eyes, nose and the mouth line with Pure Black.
5. Shade the Bears bow with Burnt Umber and then add some Burnt Carmine to brighten it up a tad.
6. Highlight the bow with Napthol Crimson and then some Napthol Crimson + Pure Orange.
7. Add the linework on the bow with Pure Orange + Warm White (the same peach color used earlier).

Background lettering:
1. Paint the linework behind the animals with Heartland Blue (or your choice of colors from your palette) using a liner brush.
2. Paint "Friends" above the animals with Heartland Blue. Outline the letters slightly with Payne's Gray. Let dry.

4 Finish

1. Apply one coat of Waterbase Varnish to the design area. Lightly antique the edges using Burnt Umber oil paint. Use a soft cloth to remove the desired amount of paint.
2. Remove the tape from the edges of the frame. Touch up any of the Taffy Basecoat that may have come off with the tape.
3. Apply a coat of Waterbase Varnish over all four sides of the frame. I noticed that when I did this, it crackled even more. I liked that and only mention it to caution you not to be surprised. Should it crackle a little more than you want, add a little Heartland Blue and some of the cracks will disappear.
4. Paint the small lettering around the frame with Heartland Blue. Transfer the lettering if necessary or freehand the words. There are many neat sayings for friends, I just happen to think that love and friendship go hand in hand so please adapt your own favorite saying to the border if you prefer. Let dry.
5. Antique the frame edges (where the small lettering is placed) with Burnt Umber as you did before. Don't forget to paint the inside cut edge as well.
6. Apply varnish to the entire piece. ❑

*F*ruit *P*lanter

painted by *D*onna *D*ewberry

This project appeared in Donna's first book for Plaid using her double-load painting method. The book, published in 1995, was entitled **Double-Load Painting**. *Her method is now the popular* **One-Stroke** *method.*

*D*onna is the mother of seven children and a native Floridian. She has been involved with arts and crafts all her married life, over 25 years. After many evenings at her dining room table enjoying the pleasures of decorative painting, she developed a technique for stress-free painting that is the basis for her "One Stroke" series of painting books. She seems to find peace and great pleasure in painting at her table, this being the same table where her children would share their concerns or excitement about the day's activities. The same table where she has conversed with friends and neighbors; the same table where tears of frustration have been shed; the same table where her laugher and excitement have been exclaimed – her creativity seems to shine brighter at this table.

One-Stroke Certification

For information on Donna's three-and-half-day seminar, where she teaches her painting techniques as well as how to start a business in decorative painting and provides tips for being a good teacher, how to demo in stores, and how to get your painting published, contact her one of these ways:

- *By mail:* Dewberry Designs, 125C Robin Road, Altamonte Springs, FL 32701
- *By phone:* 407-260-2508

- *By fax:* 407-831-0658
- *On the Web:* www.onestroke.com (certification and seminar information) www.thestrokingedge.com (complete

One-Stroke resource)
- *By e-mail:* dewberry@magicnet.net

One Stroke Double-Loading Technique

Dip one side of the chisel edge of dampened brush into one color.

Dip other side into second color. Colors should form triangles on the brush and meet in the middle.

Stroke brush to blend colors where they meet.

1. Wet your brush and gently tap on paper towel to remove excess water.
2. Pick up paint by dipping one corner of the brush in one color and the opposite corner of the brush in another color (for double loading).
3. Stroke brush back and forth in a sweeping motion. Repeat step 2 once or twice until the brush is full of paint two-thirds of the way up the bristles.

- When brush is loaded correctly, your strokes should feel as though the bristles glide. If the brush is coarse or splits, you do not have enough paint on the brush.
4. When you need more paint: Once your brush is loaded, all you need to do to paint is to pick up a touch of paint of either color and start painting. You do not need to brush back and forth on your palette anymore. If you continue

to do this every time you pick up paint, you will not have enough paint to finish your strokes.
- *Don't* brush back and forth on your palette every time you pick up paint – if you do, you won't have enough paint on your brush to finish your strokes.
- When loading brushes #6 and smaller, load with one color first, then sidestroke into the second color to double load.

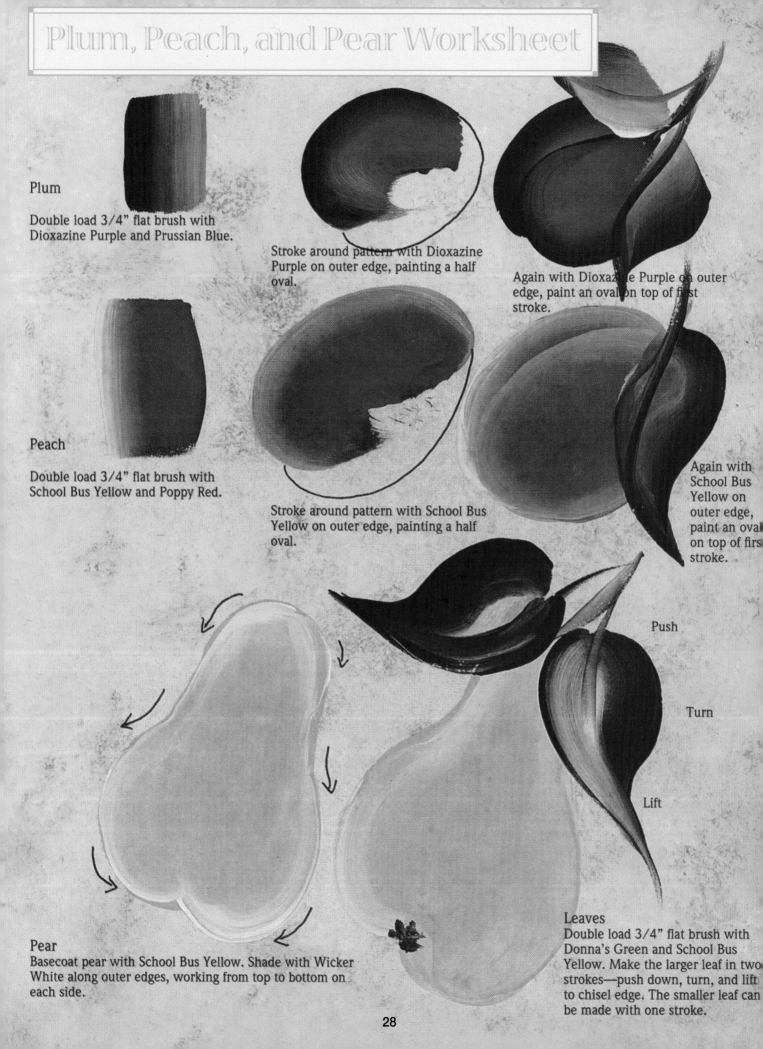

Plum

Double load 3/4" flat brush with Dioxazine Purple and Prussian Blue.

Stroke around pattern with Dioxazine Purple on outer edge, painting a half oval.

Again with Dioxazine Purple on outer edge, paint an oval on top of first stroke.

Peach

Double load 3/4" flat brush with School Bus Yellow and Poppy Red.

Stroke around pattern with School Bus Yellow on outer edge, painting a half oval.

Again with School Bus Yellow on outer edge, paint an oval on top of first stroke.

Push

Turn

Lift

Pear

Basecoat pear with School Bus Yellow. Shade with Wicker White along outer edges, working from top to bottom on each side.

Leaves

Double load 3/4" flat brush with Donna's Green and School Bus Yellow. Make the larger leaf in two strokes—push down, turn, and lift to chisel edge. The smaller leaf can be made with one stroke.

Fruit Planter

∞

By Donna Dewberry

Pictured on page 27

1 Gather These Supplies

FolkArt® Acrylic Colors:
Wicker White #901
Poppy Red #630
School Bus Yellow #736
English Mustard #959
Green Forest #448*

FolkArt® Artists' Pigments:
Burnt Umber #462
Napthol Crimson #435
Alizarin Crimson #758
Dioxazine Purple #463
Prussian Blue #486

Painting Surface
Galvanized tin oval container

Other Supplies
FolkArt® Clear Acrylic Matte Sealer

Mid-size Brushes:
3/4" flat #1176
Scruffy Brush #1172
Brush Set #1171 includes: a 3/4" flat,
　#12 flat, and #2 script liner.
Brush Set #1177 includes: a #8 flat and
　a #10 flat.

2 Preparation

Prepare Tin Surface and Transfer pattern
onto surface.

3 Paint The Design

Branches
1. Double Load 3/4" flat brush with Burnt
Umber and Wicker White.
2. Paint branches using chisel edge of
brushes.
3. Allow to dry.

Pears
1. Load 3/4" flat brush with English
Mustard and basecoat pear.
2. Sideload 3/4" flat brush with Green
Forest.
3. Shade pear using photograph as guide.

Peach, Plums
1. Paint according to Plum, and Peach
Worksheet.

Apple
Paint the same as shown on Apples
Worksheet

Leaves
1. Paint Leaves with School Bus Yellow
and Green Forest. See leaves on
worksheet.

Curlicues
1. Load #2 script liner with inky Green
Forest. Paint Curlicues using tip of
brush.

Blossoms
1. Double Load 3/4" flat brush with
Wicker White and English Mustard.
2. Paint blossoms with a combination of
c-strokes and dabbing.
3. Allow to dry.

4 Finish

1. Spray with two coats of Matte Acrylic
Sealer. ❑

*＊ Green Forest is referred to as "Donna's Green"
on worksheet.*

**Pattern – Enlarge 200%
for actual size**

$\mathcal{B}$ird Nest & $\mathcal{E}$ggs

painted by $\mathcal{D}$orothy $\mathcal{E}$gan

*This wonderful step stool was published in **Baskets of Beauty**. This was Dorothy's first book for Plaid. The design can be painted on other items – canvas or boxes.*

$\mathcal{D}$orothy Egan has been involved in various forms of art and crafts most of her life, and has been painting and teaching for over thirty years. She began teaching "minis" at a shop named "The Apple Barrel" before joining "The Oil Rig", a group of four teachers who combined their talents in seminars and books. Eventually she published her first solo book, *TAKE A GANDER* which lead to teaching many classes throughout the United States and Canada. She has gone on to publish or co-author over thirty books, including her most recent ones published by North Light Books, *PAINTING AND DECORATING BIRDHOUSES* and *HOW TO START MAKING MONEY WITH YOUR DECORATIVE PAINTING*. Dorothy has written two monthly columns for *Crafts magazine* and is a regular contributor to several other publications.

How to Paint Nests

Painting the eggs first is a change from the way most nests are painted, but there are advantages. One advantage is that the eggs can be reshaped with the dark nest colors, if needed. It also eliminates the "halo" effect around the eggs that can occur from trying to save the pattern lines. More shading and/or stronger highlights can be added to the eggs after the nest is complete.

Thin paint with water and use a long liner (script) brush to paint the nest. Work from dark to light, making fine, interweaving lines. Underpaint with the darkest value, then "build" the nest, working from dark to light. If too much light value is used and the dark values are lost, rinse the brush and add small bits of color and more linework with the dark value.

Bird Nest & Eggs

By Dorothy Egan

1 Gather These Supplies

FolkArt® Acrylic Colors:
Butter Pecan #939
Navy Blue #403

FolkArt® Artists' Pigments:
Green Umber #471
Hauser Green Medium #460
Warm White #649
Raw Sienna #452
Pure Orange #628
Yellow Ochre #917
Burnt Sienna #943
Ice Blue #457
Aqua #481
Burnt Umber #462
Brilliant Ultramarine #484
Titanium White #480
Medium Yellow #455

Painting Surface:
Wood step stool, 11-1/2" wide x 12" high
Other Supplies:
Wood sealer
FolkArt® Floating Medium #868
Foam sponge, 2" square (a 2" x 2" piece of upholstery or packing foam works well)
FolkArt® Artist Varnish, satin finish #887 or matte finish #890

2 Preparation

1. Sand stool well and wipe with tack cloth. Apply sealer. When dry, sand again lightly and wipe with tack cloth.
2. Basecoat steps only with Warm White. The remainder of the stool will be painted later. Let dry.
3. Transfer nest shape to surface.

4. Cut a 2" square of foam. Pull corners up to form a pouf. Sponge steps with subtle mixtures of Brilliant Ultramarine, Burnt Sienna, Ice Blue, and Titanium White. Carry color 1/4" to 1/2" into the nest area. Let dry.
5. Transfer pattern to surface.

3 Paint the Design

Eggs:
Refer to Nest & Egg Painting Worksheet.
1. Paint the eggs, working from dark to light. Brush-mix colors. Wipe brush between colors, but do not rinse brush except when picking up the lightest values:
Dark values: use a mix of Brilliant Ultramarine + Burnt Sienna to establish the dark values.
Medium values: without rinsing brush, pick up a touch of Aqua + more Titanium White for the middle values.
Light values: wipe the brush then pick up more Titanium White (+ a little Aqua if needed).
2. Add a final highlight with Titanium white + a pin dot of Medium Yellow.

Nests:
1. Underpaint the nest with Brilliant Ultramarine + Burnt Sienna. Carefully paint around the eggs.
2. Work Burnt Sienna + Raw Sienna into the painting at the outer edges of the nest. Allow to dry.
3. Thin paint with water and use a long liner brush for linework on the nest. Work from dark to light, making fine vine-like strokes. If you apply too much light and the nest loses it's

depth, add more linework with the dark value colors. Apply colors in the following order:
Brilliant Ultramarine + Burnt Umber
Burnt Sienna
Raw Sienna
Raw Sienna + Titanium White
Yellow Ochre + Titanium White
Pure Orange + Titanium White
Titanium White
Medium Yellow

Branch:
1. Paint the branch with Brilliant Ultramarine + Burnt Umber and Burnt Sienna.
2. Highlight with Burnt Sienna + Titanium White and Raw Sienna + Titanium White.
3. Use thinned paint on a script brush to paint vine and small branches.

Leaves:
1. Basecoat leaves with Green Umber.
2. Overstroke with Hauser Green Medium for a middle value.
3. Highlight with Hauser Green Medium + Yellow Ochre + Titanium White.
4. Use floating medium to add tints of Burnt Sienna to some of the leaves.

Feather (on lower step):
1. Basecoat the feather with a wash of Brilliant Ultramarine + Burnt Umber.
2. Use a fine liner to pull feather strokes from spine to tip with Titanium White. When dry, use Floating Medium to shade along the spine.
3. Shade under the feather with Brilliant Ultramarine + Burnt Umber.

Finishing Touch:
Spatter the steps with the background colors.

4 Finish

1. Paint the rest of the stool with Butter Pecan.
2. Paint the rims with Navy Blue.
3. When dry, finish with several coats of matte or satin waterbase varnish. ❏

Pattern – Enlarge 200% for actual size

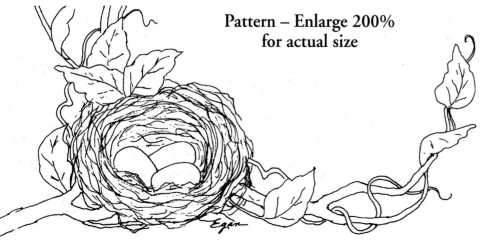

Nest & Egg Painting Worksheet

Eggs:

Use Brilliant Ultramarine + Burnt Sienna + Titanium White to establish dark values.

Without rinsing brush, work into Brilliant Ultramarine + Aqua + Titanium White for middle values.

Finishing painting eggs with Aqua + Titanium White for the light value. Highlight eggs with Titanium White + Medium Yellow.

Nest:

Underpaint nest with Brilliant Ultramarine + Burnt Sienna, painting around eggs. Work into Brunt Sienna at outer edges, Keep edges soft.

Use a script brush and thin paint with water. Begin linework with Brilliant Ultramarine + Burnt Umber. Add strokes of Burnt Sienna, Raw Sienna + Titanium White, Yellow Ochre + Titanium White, Pure Orange + Titanium White, Titanium White, Medium Yellow.

Branch:

Establish the dark values of branches with Brilliant Ultramarine + Burnt Sienna, Burn Umber.

Add more linework with Burnt Sienna + Raw Sienna + Titanium White. Add middle values with Burnt Sienna, Raw Sienna.

Highlight branch with Raw Sienna + Titanium White.

*P*ansy *B*ox

painted by *G*inger *E*dwards

*Pansies symbolize thoughtfulness. This gorgeous little box was presented in **Old Fashioned Florals** published in 1997 by Plaid.*

Ginger Edwards has been painting decoratively for 29 years. She travels extensively to conduct seminars on acrylic, water-color, and oil painting. Among the many highlights of her career was a trip to teach in Japan. Author of numerous painting instruction books, Ginger is also a regular contributor to national magazines. She is a member of the *National Society of Decorative Painters* and served as its' president in 1988-89. Ginger received the Distinguished Service Award from the NSTDP in 1990. In 1991 she received the Society's highest honor, the Silver Palette Award.

You may contact this artist at:
Ginger Edwards
2136 Memorial Drive
Alexandria, LA 71301
Phone 318-448-8726
Fax 318-443-4473

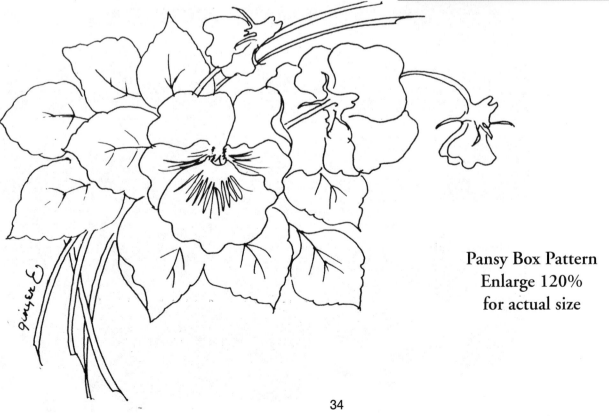

Pansy Box Pattern
Enlarge 120%
for actual size

Pansy Box

∽

By Ginger Edwards

1 Gather These Supplies

FolkArt® Acrylic Colors:
Periwinkle #404
Violet Pansy #440
Night Sky #443
Thunder Blue #609
Honeycomb #942
Wicker White #901
Thicket #924
Lemon Custard #735
Lime Yellow #478
Lemonade #904
Ivory White #427

Painting Surfaces
Oblong Bentwood Box

Other Supplies
Liner Brushes size 1, and 10/0
Flat Brushes sizes #2,#8,#10,#12
Mop Brush size 1" (optional)
Dagger Brush size 1/4" (optional)
1" sponge brush
FolkArt® Thicker #948
FolkArt® Waterbase Varnish #791
First Step Wood Sealer

2 Preparation

1. With sponge brush, basecoat outside and inside of box bottom and inside box lid with Periwinkle + First Step Wood Sealer (1:1 ratio). Let dry. Sand Lightly. Apply second coats if necessary. Let dry.
2. Transfer design to box lid with gray transfer paper.

3 Paint The Design

Basecoating
1. Leaves, stems, and calyxes: Basecoat light areas with Lime Yellow and dark areas with Lime Yellow + Thicket.
2. Yellow pansy and top two petals of purple pansy: Basecoat light areas with Ivory White and darker areas with Ivory White + Lemon Custard.
3. Bottom three petals of purple pansy and buds: Ivory White + a small amount of Violet Pansy.
4. Let paint dry before continuing.

Leaves
1. Shade with Thicket + Thunder Blue.
2. Highlight with Lime Yellow + Lemonade.
3. Add brightest highlights with Ivory White added to the highlight mix above.
4. Veins: Lime Yellow + Lemonade.

Purple Pansy
1. Shade bottom three petals with Violet Pansy + Night Sky.
2. Sparingly highlight these petals with Ivory White + Thunder Blue.
3. Sparingly tint edges of top two petals with Violet Pansy and/or Violet Pansy + a bit of Honeycomb.
4. Highlight these petals with Lemonade and/or Lemonade + Wicker White.

Buds
1. Shade with Violet Pansy + Night Sky.
2. Tint sparingly with Lemon Custard.
3. Highlight sparingly with Wicker White + a speck of Violet Pansy.

Yellow Pansy
1. Shade with Honeycomb. Deepen shading sparingly with Thunder Blue + Thicket.
2. Tint with Honeycomb + Violet Pansy.
3. Highlight with Lemonade, then with Lemonade + Wicker White.
4. Paint a stamen in center of throat with Thicket. Highlight stamen with Lime Yellow.
5. Paint dark markings on petals with Violet Pansy + Night Sky.
6. Stipple a little fuzz on the edges of the two main petals beside the throat with lemonade.

Calyxes and Stems
1. Shade with same color as for leaves
2. Highlight with same color as for leaves.

Background
1. After all paint is thoroughly dry, erase any visible pattern lines.
2. Tint color onto the background around the design. Use any or all of the following colors: Lemonade, Violet Pansy, Periwinkle, and Thunder Blue + Thicket. A mop brush works well for this.
3. Spatter lightly with Periwinkle.
4. Use a moistened cotton swab to remove any of this paint that you might have brushed onto the flowers or leaves. Let paint dry.

4 Finish

1. Paint a narrow line around the box lid 1/4" from edge with Periwinkle. A 1/4" dagger brush works great for this. Let dry.
2. Varnish inside and outside of box with waterbase varnish. ❑

Pansy Painting Worksheet

Step 1:
First paint both flowers and leaves using two values of paint.
Blend the colors while still wet. Allow the paint to dry after
this step.

Step 2:
Add the shading. Only a small amount of paint is
necessary to create a soft tint and shading. Notice
how greater dimension in the painting results from
this step. Allow paint to dry after this step.

Step 3:
Finish the painting by strengthening shading and tints
as desired.
Stroke highlights on petals from the edges towards the
center of the flower. Stroke highlights on leaves from
the center vein area towards the edges.
Add details using a liner brush.
After all paint is dry, erase any visible pattern lines. Tint
the background with soft colors to enhance the design.

Church Picnic

painted by John Gutcher

*John Gutcher's carefully thought out and illustrated techniques will inspire you to paint this lovely Picnic Basket. This book entitled **Beginner's Guide to Landscape Painting** was published in 1998 by Plaid Enterprises, Inc.*

J ohn Gutcher is an award winning Portrait/mural painter, instructor, and demonstrator for manufacturer's products. He teaches weekly oil and acrylic painting classes at his Tampa studio/gallery. He also travels widely, teaching painting at workshops and conventions throughout the U.S.

John's oil paintings and Portraits have won numerous national, state, and local awards and may be found in many private collections throughout this country and Canada. Reproductions of his commercial and fine art have been used for advertising and for limited edition prints, cards, and book covers. His unique design and decorative pieces have won national awards and have been published in *Artists of Florida, PaintWorks, PaintWorks Special Christmas Issue, PaintWorks Holiday Angels, Let's Paint, Painting, Decorative Artists Workbook,* and *The Decorative Painter.* He has also appeared on television, most notably on PBS, and has eight videos with *Perfect Palette.* His designs are now being published in pattern packets so that other painters may benefit from his experience.

In addition to all this, John has found time to participate in community projects, such as painting altar murals for churches and outdoor murals for municipalities in his area. ❏

John Gutcher's Painting Style

John's landscapes are painted in a very loose style using a painterly technique. The blending is accomplished by mixing multiple hues on the palette. Then they are applied to the surface in strokes, brush blending them as you paint. Most of the subjects use multiple layers of paint. These are laid on first in massive large shapes to establish the color composition and value placement. Then additional layers of paint are applied to break the massive shapes to smaller ones, and then still smaller ones, until the final detail is established. John tends to work the entire composition at one time, to develop the depth and aerial perspective in the landscape.

Leaf Clusters

(1) (2) (3)

Light Source

Tree Clusters

(1) (2) (3)

Light Source

Tree Trunk and Branches

(1) (2)

Light Source

Open Sky Spaces

Hauser Green Dark

Hauser Light Green

Hauser Green Medium

Hauser Light Green + White

TREES
Worksheet #1

Leaf Clusters

1. Outline leaf cluster with white charcoal pencil. When painting leaves, keep edges soft, loose and irregularly shaped. Remember that the light source is coming from the upper right. Use a deerfoot stipple brush to tap in underneath shadows using Hauser Green Dark.
2. Tap in middle values slightly overlapping shadows with Hauser Green Medium.
3. Tap in highlight values slightly overlapping middle values with Hauser Green Light.

Tree Clusters

1. Outline shape of the tree with white charcoal pencil. Paint general shape of the tree trunk and main branches with Raw Umber. Use deerfoot stipple brush to tape in bottom left shadows with Hauser Green Dark. Include tree's shadow.
2. Tape in middle value with Hauser Green Medium + a touch of Titanium White overlapping dark values slightly. Place some of this on ground under tree on both the left and right sides.
3. Tap in light values on top right side with Hauser Green Light, overlapping middle values slightly. Add Titanium White for lighter green highlights. Using liner brush, paint in grass highlights on right side only.

Tree Trunk and Branches

1. Using liner brush with Raw Umber, paint shape of trunk and main branches darker on bottom left sides, lighter on upper right sides. Pull stroke out from main branch in short jagged strokes. Hesitate slightly with brush to create knot in branch, change directions slightly, then proceed with next branch. Tiny twigs on ends of branches are almost straight, short thin lines. With a white charcoal pencil, lightly indicate leaf cluster with circles and ovals. Large oval in center indicates open area for birds to fly through. Leave open areas throughout tree pattern where sky and branches show.
2. Tap in leaf clumps as above starting with dark shadow on lower left sides of each cluster, Hauser Green Medium overlapping Hauser Green Dark, then Hauser Green Light on upper right side of tree, overlapping the Hauser Green Medium slightly. ❏

**Enlarge 200%
for actual size**

41

Church Picnic

∞

By John Gutcher

1 Gather These Supplies

FolkArt® Acrylic Colors:
Butter Pecan #939
Ivory White #427

FolkArt® Artists' Pigments:
Titanium White #480
Portrait #422
True Burgundy #456
Payne's Gray #477
Dioxazine Purple #463
Cobalt Blue #720
Burnt Umber #462
Pure Orange #628
Hauser Dark Green #461
Hauser Light Green #459
Burnt Sienna #943
Medium Yellow #455
Warm White #649
Raw Sienna #452

Brushes:
#6 Flat
#2 Flat
Liner Brush
#2 Round

Other Supplies:
Picnic basket with flat wooden lid
Graphite Transfer Paper
Stylus
Sea Sponge
Blending Gel Medium #867

2 Preparation

1. Base top with Ivory White.
2. Sponge outside edge with combinations of Butter Pecan and Raw Sienna. Create a smooth vignette frame of these colors about 1/2" wide.
3. Transfer pattern to surface with graphite paper and stylus.

3 Paint the Design

Clouds and Background:
1. Begin close to light source painting clouds with Titanium White + Portrait.
2. Shadow clouds with True Burgundy + Titanium White. (See "Cloud" worksheets for details.) Use Blending Gel Medium to allow more blending time.
3. Underpaint light cool colors behind trees and foliage.
4. Tap in background trees and bushes with Payne's Gray + Titanium White, Dioxazine Purple + Titanium White , and Cobalt Blue + Titanium White. Keep all background values muted and soft.
5. With larger flat brush, create cool riverbank shadows with light grays, blues and purples.
6. On right, add shadows where needed.
7. Continue this soft gray around front and tap blend into vignette border.

Adding Details:
1. Draw varying sized tree trunks with Burnt Umber.
2. Tap in shadows of tree clusters.
3. Outline rock shadows with Burnt Umber + Titanium White.
4. Add more Titanium White for rock highlights.
5. Add another row of grass in front of rocks.
6. Add more rocks at left as shown. Use Burnt Umber for shadows, Burnt Sienna for middle values, Burnt Sienna + Titanium White for highlights. Larger rocks in foreground are darker with more contrast.

Trees Near Church:
1. Behind church, tap in medium and light value shapes for leaf clusters.
2. Values will be darker near bottom of trees and beside church.

Church:
1. Base church roof with Burnt Sienna.
2. For shadow side of church and steeple use Payne's Gray + Titanium White.
3. Use Medium Yellow for windows and door.
4. Base front of church with Warm White + touch of Burnt Sienna.
5. With chisel edge of flat brush, tap in cool grays on roof, letting brown show through for shingle effect.
6. With liner brush, shadow under eaves, steeple and windows; shadow shape of door and circular window.
7. Brighten lights in windows and door with Pure Orange.

Pathway and Bridge:
1. Continue warm colors of path leading from church toward bridge and foreground.
2. Use chisel edge of flat brush to tap in path texture with Burnt Sienna + Titanium White in varying values. Keep strokes horizontal.
3. Make upper portion of bridge lighter, lower portion darker.

At the Creek:
1. Detail creek with blues and Payne's Gray using horizontal. tapping strokes to create texture of water.
2. Paint shadow side of bridge cool colors as base, then add details of rocks darker at top light edge, lighter in lower areas.

Grass and Shrubs:
1. Paint grass with varying colors of brush-mixed greens, grays, and browns.
2. Darken shadow shrubs behind church and around path to bridge.

Foreground Grass and Flowers:
1. With liner brush, stroke varying colors and values of green foliage.
2. Pull clumps of grass over rocks and path for depth.
3. Add touches of Medium Yellow, Pure Orange, and Titanium White for a few flowers in foreground.
4. Darken shadows at base of grass clumps.

Final Touches:
1. With brush loaded with Blending Gel Medium and Payne's Gray, glaze over front shadows to form cool shadows projecting from light source.
2. Glaze a few cool shadows from large grass clumps over path and rocks. ❏

TREE TRUNKS AND BRANCHES
Worksheet #2

TREE BRANCHES

Paint branches with Raw Umber. Note that some of the branches will begin from the center of the main branch and some will begin from the sides of the main branch.

1. Stroke a fairly straight line, stop with brush still on surface, change directions slightly, continue with another short stroke, stop, repeat as needed. Toward outer areas, stroke will get thinner and shorter for smaller twigs.
2. The light source is coming from the upper right. Highlight upper right edge and darken lower left of each branch. Vertical branches don't necessarily have either shadows or highlights.

TREE TRUNK

1. Outline trunk with Raw Umber, darkening shadow areas of trunk on left side. Trunk is thicker near ground, gradually gets thinner toward sky. Add interest to boring straight tree trunks with splits, knots, curves or exposed root systems.
2. Paint middle values with Raw Sienna.
3. Highlight upper right side with Raw Sienna + Titanium White.
4. Pull some curved grass blades over tree roots to create dimension.

LARGE BRANCHES

1. Draw main branch with Raw Umber.
2. With the light source coming from upper right, use Hauser Green Dark shadows in large clusters of leaves. Use Hauser Green Medium, then Hauser Green Light in upper right of leaf clusters.
3. Accent lower left darks with Payne's Gray for additional contrast.

When looking up at a large tree branch, you will see the branch as being quite dark against the lighter sky, This is referred to as back lighting. When that same branch merges into a darker shadow area of the tree it becomes lighter than the shadow. By making a few artistic decisions like this, you can actually create more realism. Many tree trunks and branches are lighter than their backgrounds. ❑

#1- Payne's Gray
#2- Raw Sienna
#3- Raw Umber
#4- Titanium White

Tree Branches

Tree Trunk

Light Source

Light Source

Light Branches

Light Background

#1   #2   #3   #4

Large Branches

Dark Shadows

Dark Branches

$\mathcal{P}$recious $\mathcal{K}$itty

painted by Peggy Harris

*Even if you've never painted animals you'll be amazed at the results when you use these unique techniques. This irresistible kitty was born in **Adorable Baby Animals**.*

$\mathcal{A}$ graduate of the University of Kansas, Peggy Harris has been a professional wildlife painter for 33 years. To keep up with the demand for her paintings of baby animals, Peggy developed the Harris Method – a systematic method for painting realistic fur and feathers in a modicum of time, using non-traditional techniques and materials.

Thousands of artists have enjoyed *Peggy Harris' Paintable Kingdom* on public television and her book and videotape, *Painting Baby Animals with Peggy Harris*, published by North Light. Many have traveled to Nashville, Tenn. to participate in her workshops and seminars. A book specifically for decorative painters, *Peggy Harris' Baby Animals to Paint and Cherish*, also published by North Light, is also available.

If you love to paint and love animals, Peggy's method is for you. You can do it – come share the love!

You can contact this artist at:

Peggy Harris,
P. O. Box 784,
Antioch, TN 37011.

15 Terms to Know

Airplane: To lift off or onto the painting surface gradually and smoothly with a cotton swab or brush, as if the swab or brush were an airplane and the surface is the runway.

Bright brush: A paint brush with a flat ferrule and a chiseled square tip similar to a flat brush. Here it always refers to a synthetic hair brush used either for painting or lifting out paint.

Bristle brush: Here it always refers to a **round** natural white bristle brush used to create fur or feathers as it is stroked through the paint pattern.

Double load: To paint with two colors side by side on a brush.

Dry cotton swab: A fresh cotton swab with no water or paint in it.

Fall off (the brush): Allowing paint to flow from the brush to the painting surface without letting the hairs of the brush touch the underlying paint or the surface.

Glow: I use "glow" as a verb, It is the technique of creating a subtle highlight by lifting out paint with a cotton swab or brush. You can "dry glow" by lifting out paint with a dry cotton swab or brush. Or, you can "wet glow" to create the illusion of light in an area by lifting out paint with a wet cotton swab or brush.

Rake: *In this book,* an oval tipped, thin haired filbert brush used for fur and grass; also called a grass comb.

Re-brush: To perfect a previously brushed area of fur with a bristle brush; usually refers to brushing a glowed area.

Rotation (of fur): Brushing fur in an orderly sequence of angles as it layers over the body.

Rough brush: The first brushing of layers of fur using a bristle brush or a rake to blend the paint pattern.

Scrumble: Invented word meaning a "scruffy jumble" of paint used in the paint pattern. Implies squiggly strokes, loosely applied.

Stipple: To tap the bristle brush rapidly on the paint pattern with all brush tips hitting the surface.

Wet brush: A bright synthetic hair brush that has been dipped in water and squeezed out or wiped clean, but still holds enough moisture to lift out paint from the surface.

Wet cotton swab: A cotton swab that has been dipped in water and blotted on a paper towel pad.

Precious Kitty

by Peggy Harris

1 Gather These Supplies

FolkArt® Acrylic Colors:
Silver Sterling (metallic) #662

FolkArt® Artists' Pigments:
Asphaltum #476
Burnt Sienna #943
Medium Yellow #455
Pure Black #479
Raw Umber #485
Red Light #629
Titanium White #480
Turner's Yellow #679

Project Surface:
Octagonal flat lid wooden box, 7"

Other Supplies:
FolkArt® Blending Gel Medium #867
FolkArt® Glazing Medium #693
FolkArt® Floating Medium #868
Scotch® brand Magic Tape
Optional: Craft knife

2 Make Color Mixes

- **Yellow base mix** - Titanium White + Turner's Yellow + Medium Yellow + Raw Umber
- **Pewter mix** - Titanium White + Pure Black + Medium Yellow + Burnt Sienna
- **Pink ear and nose mix** - Titanium White + Red Light

3 Prepare

1. Prepare the box, following instructions in the "Preparation & Finishing" section.
2. Apply gesso to the lid. Let dry.
3. Base paint the box with the yellow base color.
4. Mix equal amounts Asphaltum and Glazing Medium. Lightly antique the box. Let dry.
5. Trace the design and transfer with gray transfer paper.
6. Undercoat the kitty and pussy willow bud areas with Titanium White. (The pattern should show through.) "Sand" the undercoat with a piece of a brown paper bag. Wipe away dust.

4 Paint the Kitty

Apply Blending Gel Medium, glow, and re-brush only as much of the kitty as you can complete before the paint dries. After finishing one small section, move to an adjacent area and repeat the steps. After all areas of the kitty have been glowed and re-brushed, let dry. You can enhance the design by glazing with successive layers of paint and Blending Gel Medium. See the Kitty Worksheet and the directional arrows on the pattern for guidance.

The Fur:
1. The Paint Pattern - Apply Blending Gel Medium over the area with a bright brush. While wet, paint the black shadows and fur patterns. Loosely scrumble in pewter color, stroking in the direction the fur grows. Paint with Titanium White around the eyes, on the forehead and muzzle, and under the chin.
2. The Rough Brush - Using a bristle brush and no pressure, brush through the paint pattern with back and forth strokes to create layers of fur. Quickly refine the edge fur with a filbert rake before the paint dries, then continue to brush the interior fur. Add paint as needed. Stipple short muzzle fur.
3. Glow with Titanium White - Blend Titanium White into the brushed fur with a bristle brush. Do not overblend.
4. Re-brush and Groom - Continue brushing Pure Black shadows and Titanium White highlights on the fur with a filbert rake. Clean and re-load the brush often. Extend the edge fur with wispy hairs, using a script brush with the pewter color. Let dry.

Remaining Kitty Details:
1. Apply Blending Gel Medium over the dry fur. Paint in blend in more layers of fur. Repeat as many times as you wish. Airplane your brushes for delicate fur tips.
2. Apply Blending Gel to the ears and add feathery white fur, using a filbert rake and a script brush.
3. Paint the eyes and nose, following the steps on the Kitty Worksheet.
4. Paint and shade whisker dots. Paint whiskers with a script brush. *Option:* Scratch off with a craft knife.

5 Paint Remainder of Design

Pussy Willows:
Paint, then fuzz the pussy willows with a bristle brush, following the steps on the Kitty Worksheet.

Silver Band:
1. Mask the band around the lid with tape.
2. Paint with several coats Silver Sterling. Remove tape. Let dry.

6 Finish

1. Varnish the box with several coats of varnish. **Don't** sand between the first two coats; sanding could abrade the delicate fur lines. Let last coat dry completely.
2. Apply Painter's Finishing Wax to bring out the beauty of the painting and prevent the lid from sticking. ❑

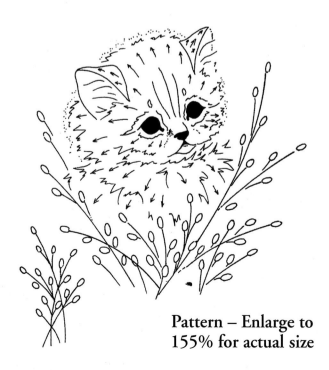

Pattern – Enlarge to 155% for actual size

Kitty Worksheet

The Paint Pattern
Paint with a bright brush.

Pewter mix

The Rough Brush
Create fur with a bristle brush.

Pure Black

Titanium White

Glow some areas with White.
Brush in Titanium White,
using a bristle brush.

Re-brush and Groom
Groom with a filbert rake.

Enhance darks

Use script brush
for wispy hairs.

Perfect
eye fur

Add more layers

Layering colors with Blending Gel over
dry kitty may be repeated over and over
for many layers.

Finish ear
fur.

Add more layers

Eye:
Raw Umber

Blend in
Titanium White

Add Pure
Black pupil

Highlight with
Titanium White

Pink mix

Pewter mix

Accent with
Pure Black

Pussy Willows:

Paint
Raw
Umber
stem
lightly.

Pewter
mix

Raw
Umber

harris

47

Bird's Nest Birdhouse

painted by Priscilla Hauser

*The inspiration for this project came from an old birdhouse hanging from a big oak tree outside of Priscilla's Tulsa Oklahoma studio. She first painted this Birdhouse for the book titled **Bird Palaces**.*

She's the "first lady of decorative painting," with good reason. Due to Priscilla Hauser's efforts, dreams, and ability to draw people to her, the first meeting of the National Society of Tole and Decorative Painters took place October 22, 1972. Since that first meeting, attended by Priscilla and 21 others, the organization has thrived, and so has Priscilla.

From her beginning efforts as a tole painter in the early 1960s, when she took classes at a YMCA in Raytown, Missouri, Priscilla Hauser has become a world-renowned teacher and author and the decorative painting industry's ambassador to the world. She has traveled to teach in Canada, Japan, Argentina, and The Netherlands and has instructed extensively throughout the United States and at her Studio by the Sea in Panama City Beach, Florida. Besides teaching, Priscilla has illustrated her techniques through books, magazine articles, videos, and television. The results of her teaching program have led to an accreditation program for teachers.

Currently, Priscilla is spokeswoman for FolkArt® paints. She is planning all manner of wonderful things to promote these high-quality paints as well as developing new products.

Priscilla Hauser Seminars

"I can teach you to paint," says Priscilla. "Come paint with me in my beautiful Studio by the Sea! You will learn the basics: brush strokes, double loading, blending, and proper preparation of surfaces. You'll even learn some pen-and-ink techniques and some fabric painting."

Priscilla's seminars are extremely valuable to the beginner as well the more advanced painter. Her methods teach the newcomer and strengthen the experienced. The seminars last five-and-a-half days and, after studying for 100 hours, you can become accredited with the Priscilla Hauser Program.

To receive seminar details, send for Priscilla Hauser's Seminar Brochure and Schedule, P.O. Box 521013, Tulsa, OK 75152-1013.

49

Bird's Nest Birdhouse

By Priscilla Hauser

1 Gather These Supplies

FolkArt® Acrylic Colors:
Buttercream #614
Teal #405

FolkArt® Artists' Pigments:
Raw Sienna #452
Burnt Sienna #943
Titanium White #480
Pure Black #479
Burnt Umber #462
Ice Blue #457
Hauser Light Green #459
Hauser Medium Green #460
Hauser Dark Green #461
Medium Yellow #455
Warm White #649

Painting Surface:
Rustic wood and metal birdhouse

Other Supplies:
FolkArt® Waterbase Varnish

2 Preparation

1. Sand lightly. Wipe with a tack cloth.
2. Trace and transfer the design.

3 Paint the Design

See Bird's Nest Painting Worksheet and Leaves Painting Worksheet. Be prepared to sacrifice your brushes. Painting on a surface this rough will destroy a good brush, but the finished effect is worth it.

Bird's Nest:
1. Apply Blending Gel Medium. Basecoat with Raw Sienna.
2. Double load brush with Raw Sienna and Burnt Umber. Blend on palette. Shade nest.
3. Using a liner brush with thinned Burnt Umber, paint many thin lines to create straw.
4. Add thin lines of Buttercream.
5. Add thin lines of Warm White. Let dry.
6. To shade behind eggs, double load brush with Floating Medium and Burnt Umber + a touch of Raw Sienna. Blend on palette. Apply shadow.

Eggs:
1. Apply Blending Gel Medium. Basecoat with Ice Blue.
2. Double load brush with Ice Blue + a tiny touch of Burnt Umber. Blend on palette. Shade eggs.
3. Add highlights with Warm White. Let dry.
4. Double load with Floating Medium and a little Teal. Highlight the tops of the eggs.

Branches:
1. Basecoat with Warm White.
2. Shade with Burnt Umber, Burnt Sienna #943, and Pure Black.
3. Create the texture of bark with touches of thinned Buttercream and thinned Warm White.

Leaves:
Paint leaves, using the photo as a guide for color values and following the examples on the Leaf Worksheet and the instructions on page 52. Let dry.

Tendrils:
Add tendrils with Burnt Umber. Let dry.

4 Finish

Varnish **only** the painted design areas with Waterbase Varnish. ❏

Painting Worksheet
Bird's Nest

Nest:

1. Basecoat the nest with Raw Sienna.

2. Shade or float with Burnt Umber.

3. Add dark linework with thinned Burnt Umber and Burnt Sienna.

4. Add light linework with Moon Yellow and Warm White.

Eggs:

1. Basecoat with Ice Blue. Shade with Burnt Umber.

2. Highlight with Warm White.

3. Shade with Teal. Add additional highlights with Warm White.

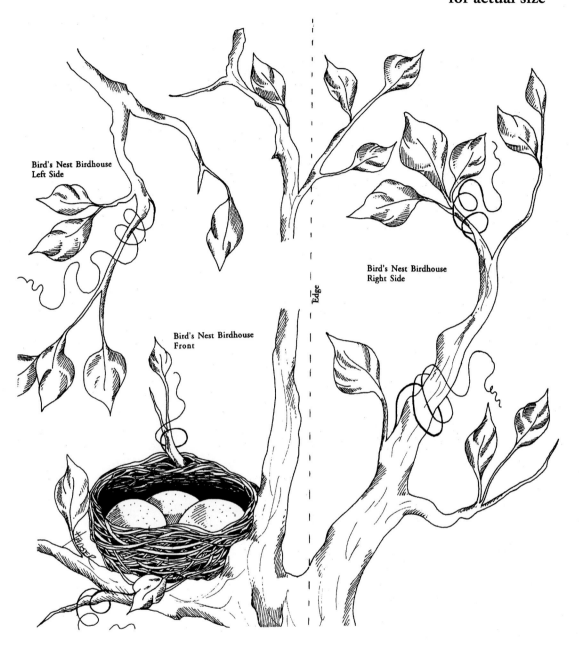

**Bird's Nest Birdhouse
Pattern
Enlarge 175%
for actual size**

Bird's Nest Birdhouse
Left Side

Bird's Nest Birdhouse
Right Side

Bird's Nest Birdhouse
Front

Edge

Hints From Priscilla

- Acrylic paints like to be cold. They won't dry as quickly if the room temperature is 68 degrees or colder. Heat dries, cold does not.

- Do not allow air to blow on your project while you're painting. Moving air rapidly dries acrylic paint. Still air allows you more time to move the paint.

- Put ice in the water under your palette. The coldness will help the acrylics stay wet longer.

- Humidity keeps things wet. The higher the humidity, the more time you'll have for blending.

- Use a lot of paint so the colors will blend together.

- If you blend too long and the paint begins to dry, it could lift. Always work as quickly as possible.

Leaves Painting Worksheet

By Priscilla Hauser

The Leaf Worksheet shows how to paint a leaf with five basic brush strokes and uses a simple dry brush blending technique.

Leaves are painted in different values. In decorative painting, we don't paint with an established light source because we are painting around and over the tops of objects. When we paint a group of leaves, the leaves at the back of the design are painted in a dark value. The leaves in the middle are painted in a medium value, and the leaves closest to the front of the design are painted the lightest. The three values are illustrated on the worksheet.

*I suggest painting 50 of each type before you paint a project. Beautiful leaves take time and practice. Please find the time to practice. Once you become comfortable painting leaves, take artistic license and add touches of the colors of your choice. It is important to have contrast within the leaves **and** between the leaves.*

1 Undercoating

If you are painting on a sealed or painted background, it may be necessary to undercoat the leaf. (On an unsealed surface, undercoating may not be necessary.) Undercoat dark value leaves with Hauser Dark Green, medium value leaves with Hauser Medium Green, and light value leaves with Hauser Light Green. Paint the five strokes as shown on the worksheet, fill in the center, and let dry before proceeding.

2 Color Palettes for Leaves

Each leaf value has it own palette. A touch of Hauser Dark Green may be used in the base or shadow area of each leaf so the leaves are color-coordinated with each other.

Dark Leaf:
Hauser Dark Green #461
Burnt Umber #462
Ice Blue #457
Hauser Light Green #459

Medium Leaf:
Hauser Medium Green #460
Burnt Umber #462
Hauser Light Green #459
Medium Yellow #455
Titanium White #480

Light Leaf:
Hauser Light Green #459
Burnt Umber #462
Titanium White #480
Yellow Light #918

3 Painting Basic Leaves

Though the colors vary from leaf to leaf, the techniques for painting all leaves are the same. See the Leaf Worksheet for colors and strokes. A #6 flat brush was used.

1. Apply Blending Gel Medium to the leaf.
2. Double load brush as listed below. Blend on palette. Apply the shadow at the point where the leaf goes under another leaf, a flower, or an object. See Leaf Worksheet, Step 1.
   Dark Leaf: Hauser Dark Green and Burnt Umber
   Medium Leaf: Hauser Medium Green and Burnt Umber
   Light Leaf: Hauser Light Green and Burnt Umber
3. Paint the first stroke, then the second stroke, then the third stroke. See Leaf Worksheet, Steps 2 and 3. Use a generous amount of paint. Pick up more paint as needed.
4. Double load brush as listed below. Blend on palette. Paint strokes 4 and 5. Be sure to angle your brush as shown. See Leaf Worksheet, Step 4.
   Dark Leaf: Hauser Dark Green and Ice Blue
   Medium Leaf: Hauser Medium Green and Titanium White #480
   Light Leaf: Hauser Light Green and Titanium White #480
5. Apply colors listed below to center of leaf. Use generous amounts of paint. See Leaf Worksheet, Step 5.
   Dark Leaf: Hauser Light Green and Ice Blue
   Medium Leaf: Hauser Light Green and Medium Yellow #455
   Light Leaf: Yellow Light and Titanium White #480
6. Wipe the brush and blend out into each of the five strokes. **Use a light touch.** If you press too hard, you'll muddy the colors. See Step 6.
7. Lightly blend back from the outside edges of the leaf toward the base. Pick up Blending Gel Medium on your brush if paint seems to be drying out. See Step 7. If needed, accent the edges with Ice Blue to create contrast.
8. Using the flat edge of a flat brush or a liner brush with Burnt Umber, paint the veins. See Step 8.

4 Painting Ivy Leaves

Ivy leaves are leaves with three sections. Ivy leaves can be painted in dark, medium, or light values using the same techniques and colors as basic leaves. The ivy leaf is illustrated on the Leaf Worksheet. Here are the basic steps:
1. Undercoat leaf. Let dry.
2. Apply Blending Gel Medium.
3. Stroke in leaf shape.
4. Stroke in shadows.
5. Apply colors to center.
6. Lightly blend.
7. Add veins with Burnt Umber.

Leaf Worksheet

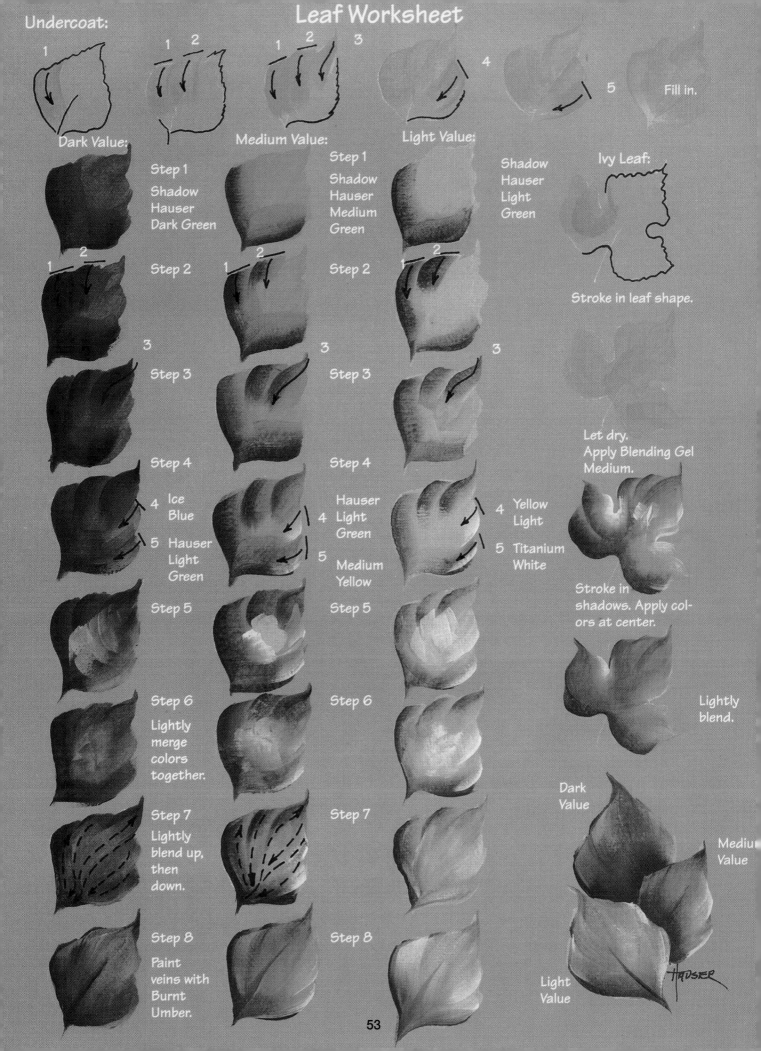

Undercoat:

1 2 1 2 3 4 5 Fill in.

Dark Value:

Step 1
Shadow
Hauser
Dark Green

Step 2

Step 3

Step 4

4 Ice Blue

5 Hauser Light Green

Step 5

Step 6
Lightly merge colors together.

Step 7
Lightly blend up, then down.

Step 8
Paint veins with Burnt Umber.

Medium Value:

Step 1
Shadow
Hauser
Medium Green

Step 2

Step 3

Step 4

4 Hauser Light Green

5 Medium Yellow

Step 5

Step 6

Step 7

Step 8

Light Value:

Step 1
Shadow
Hauser
Light Green

Step 2

Step 3

Step 4

4 Yellow Light

5 Titanium White

Shadow
Hauser
Light
Green

Ivy Leaf:

Stroke in leaf shape.

Let dry.
Apply Blending Gel Medium.

Stroke in shadows. Apply colors at center.

Lightly blend.

Dark Value

Medium Value

Light Value

Hauser

53

*P*ansy *W*atercolor painted by *L*ouise *J*ackson, M.D.A.

These beautiful pansies are a clear example of the distinctive style of Louise Jackson. This is a classic painting style that transcends years. This and many other stunning floral projects can be found in **Simply Flowers** *published by Plaid Enterprises, Inc. in 1995.*

*L*ouise has painted with a variety of media since 1966. Her work today is in watercolor, acrylics, and alkyds. She travels throughout the U.S.A., Canada, and Japan teaching workshops, as well as holding weeklong seminars in her own studio.

Louise has hosted a television series, "Painting With Louise," and has made several videos. In addition, she has authored 18 other painting instruction books.

In 1991, Louise received her Master Decorative Artist degree from the Society of Decorative Painters. She is a member of several chapters as well as the Kentucky and Ohio Watercolor Societies and the American Society of Portrait Artists. Her work appears in many corporate collections, and several of her watercolors have been purchased for the collections of major art supply manufacturers. The Society of Decorative Painters' permanent museum collection includes three of Louise's paintings, and eight of her ornaments are in the Smithsonian Museum's Christmas collection.

Louise and her husband Ken reside in Dayton, Ohio. They are parents to four children and grandparents to three girls and one boy. You may contact This artist at:

Louise Jackson
1341 Yankee Vineyards
Centerville, OHIO 45458

Tips from Louise

I like to have a stiff board under my watercolor paper to provide support. To make one like I use, have a thin board of luan cut at least 2" larger than your favorite size papers. For a quarter sheet paper which is 11" x 15", have the board cut to 13" x 17". For anything a little larger, have a 17" x 24" board cut. This will accommodate any size up to a half sheet. Some people like to use gator board. It works fine and is fairly light. Do not use cardboard; it becomes too wet.

FolkArt® Artists' Pigments As A Substitute for Watercolor Paints

The beautiful pure colors of FolkArt® Pure Pigments make them perfect for the watercolor technique. When thinned, they become transparent, retaining their pure pigmentation. If you are used to watercolors, feel confident that you can control Artists' Pigments just as well. Most of the color names that you may be familiar with in watercolors are the same. There are some colors in the Winsor Newton Watercolor line that are different.

Watercolor Pansies

By Louise Jackson

1 Gather These Supplies

FolkArt® Acrylic Colors:
Orchid #637
Periwinkle #404
Lavender #410
Green #408
Hunter Green #406
Wicker White #901
Blue Ink #642
Red Violet #636
Aspen Green #646
Wrought Iron #925

FolkArt® Artists' Pigments:
Yellow Light #918
Dioxazine Purple #463

Painting Surface
Water Color Paper 300 lb. Cold press

Brushes:
Brush 1" flat
Round Sable Brush #8
Synthetic Bright Brush #20
Script Liner
Flat Brush #20
Fan Brush
Filbert/Synthetic Brush #6

2 Preparation

Preliminary Basing
1. Base Dioxazine Purple on the beards and on the folds of the upper pansy.
2. Base beard of lower pansy with Dioxazine Purple. Paint the folds with Red Violet.
3. Base the folds of the bud with Red Violet.
4. Place a wash of Yellow Light on the yellow leaves and a wash of Green on the green ones. Refer to photograph for color placement; the rest of the leaves will be colored in the wet stage.

Wet Stage
1. Wet all of the paper thoroughly except the flowers and painted leaves. (If some wet stage color runs on the leaves, it won't hurt them.) Place paint in background, using photograph as guide. Use Yellow Light as well as Orchid in the light area. Place orchid in other areas as well. Place some Green in background and on leaves. Cover the rest with Periwinkle. (It won't appear as dark as the photograph. You'll paint another layer later.)
2. Paint in some long loose squiggles with Periwinkle.

3 Paint The Design

Lower Flower and Bud
See the Pansy Worksheet for step-by-step color application.
1. Wet one petal. Place Orchid at the outer edge of the petal, using a #6 filbert brush. Rinse and remove most of the water from the brush and use the brush to direct the color toward the center of the flower. Let the white paper show in some areas at the edge of the petal.
2. While the petal is still wet, shade with a small amount of Red Violet. (Red Violet is the darker value; it provides accent and depth. Much of the lighter value-Orchid-will still show.)
3. Paint each petal the same way.

Upper Flower
1. Use the same technique to paint the upper flower, using Lavender and shading with Dioxazine Purple.

Flower Centers
1. Base commas and balls at center with Yellow Light. Allow to dry.
2. Sideload with Green to left side.
3. Place a highlight of Wicker White on upper right of each ball.

Background-Second Layer
1. Re-wet the background and strengthen the outer colors, using Periwinkle and a little Red Violet. Dry with a hair dryer; it will be easier to paint the leaves.

Leaves
All green leaves are painted the same way, although the colors vary. See the Pansy Worksheet. I usually paint all the strokes on the leaves by sideloading the color and placing it on dry paper. You may find it easier to shade the leaves in two steps. First, Sideload the center shading. Allow it to dry. Then dampen the dried leaf and, when the paper has lost its' shine, sideload the outside shapes
1. Shade yellow leaves with Aspen Green. Shade others with Wrought Iron or Periwinkle.
2. Paint the suggested, shadowy leaves with sideloaded Periwinkle.

4 Finish

Spattering
1. Spatter with Orchid, then with Wicker White. ❑

Pattern – Enlarge 200% for actual size

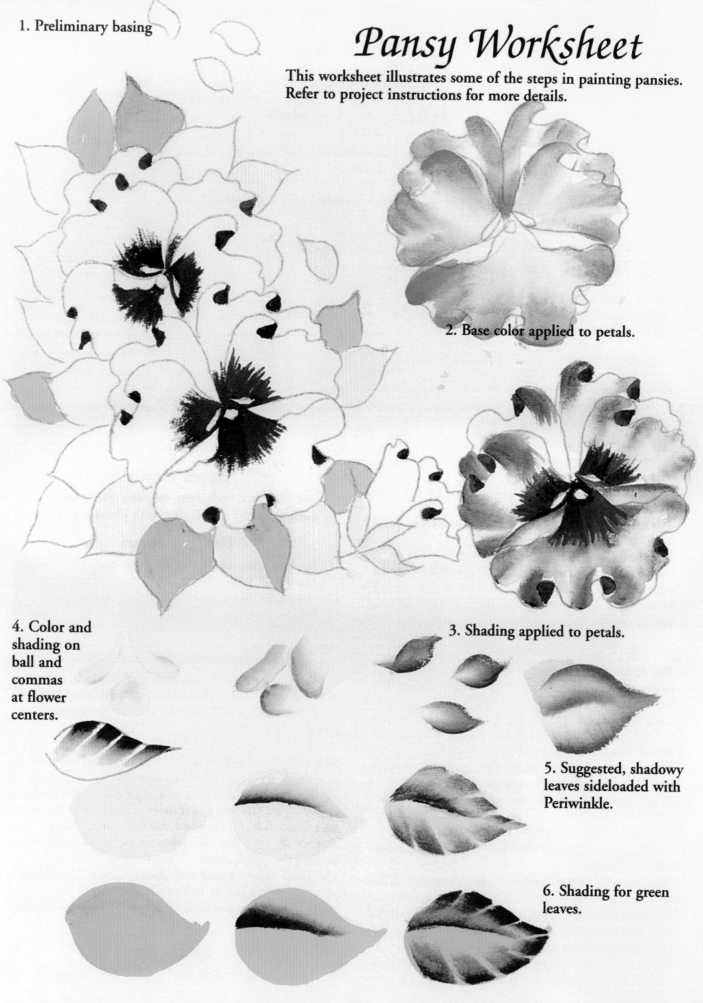

1. Preliminary basing

Pansy Worksheet

This worksheet illustrates some of the steps in painting pansies.
Refer to project instructions for more details.

2. Base color applied to petals.

3. Shading applied to petals.

4. Color and shading on ball and commas at flower centers.

5. Suggested, shadowy leaves sideloaded with Periwinkle.

6. Shading for green leaves.

Santa Ornament

painted by Linda Kiska

Linda calls Christmas "her most favorite time of year".
She created this collection of nostalgic wooden ornaments
*in a book called **Spirit of Christmas**.*

Linda tells us about herself...

Everyone needs an interest or hobby, and painting is an excellent one. I started painting in 1970 with oils. My first teacher, Virginia Jarboe, encouraged her students to be creative. I started painting with acrylics in the mid-70s and began teaching for Priscilla Hauser. Since then, painting has been my second love – family is still my first. Sometimes, it has been hard to make decisions about painting, but my husband supported me all the way. Now that we have grandchildren, my painting gets put aside more often.

Students and fellow painters have been very good to me in the past 30 years, and I have met wonderful friends through painting. I encourage you to join the National Society of Decorative Painters.

Pattern
Actual size
cut from
1/4" wood

Steps for Painting a Santa

The Painting Worksheet can be used as an illustrated guide for painting the ornament. Here are the steps I use:

1. Basecoat the pattern, using two to three coats of the basecoat color so paint is opaque. At this time I paint the back and edges of the ornament with a deep neutral color, such as Magenta, True Burgundy, or Navy Blue.

2. I dress my brush with Floating Medium, blot it lightly, and sideload it with the shading color, then float the color on the project.

3. I then apply highlighting, using the same technique used for shading.

4. After I have applied shading and highlighting, I paint the details.

5. The antique effect of the finished project comes from floating shading colors around the edges.

6. After painting is completed, I apply matte finish Artist's Varnish.

Santa Ornament

by Linda Kiska

1 Gather These Supplies

FolkArt® Acrylic Colors:
Barn Wood #936
Bluebell #909
Bright Peach #682
English Mustard #959
Evergreen #724
Licorice #938
Lipstick Red #437
Navy Blue #403
Nutmeg #944
Pure Gold (metallic) #660
Slate Blue #910
Taffy #902

FolkArt® Artists' Pigments:
Burnt Carmine #686
Burnt Sienna #943
Burnt Umber #462
Light Red Oxide #914
Payne's Gray #477
Red Light #629
Yellow Light #918

Other Supplies:
1/4" birchwood for cutting out
    ornament
2 small brass screw eyes
Small brass bell

2 Preparation

1. Cut out ornament, using pattern provided.
2. Sand edges of wood to smooth.
3. Seal wood. Let dry. Sand lightly.
4. Trace pattern and transfer to wood.

3 Paint the Design

Backgrounds of Insets:
1. Basecoat with Navy Blue. Shade with Licorice. Highlight with True Blue.
2. Paint stars in Santa inset with Taffy.
3. Spatter sky in Santa inset with Bluebell.

Trees:
1. Basecoat with Evergreen. Shade with Licorice.
2. Add linework with Pure Gold.

Santa's Face:
1. Basecoat face with Bright Peach. Shade with equal parts Nutmeg + Burnt Sienna. Highlight with Taffy.
2. Tint cheeks with Nutmeg + Red Light.
3. Paint linework on eyes with Burnt Carmine + Licorice.
4. Paint irises with Slate Blue. Shade with Licorice. Highlight with Bluebell and Taffy. Paint pupils with Licorice.
5. Paint nostrils and eyebrows with Burnt Carmine + Burnt Umber. Highlight eyebrows with Taffy.

Santa's Clothes & Hair:
1. Basecoat suit and hat with Light Red Oxide. Shade with Burnt Carmine. Highlight with Lipstick Red, then Red Light.
2. Basecoat hair and fur with Barn Wood. Shade with Payne's Gray + Burnt Umber. Highlight with Taffy.
3. Paint gloves with Evergreen. Shade with Licorice. Highlight with Evergreen + Taffy.

Santa's Bag:
1. Basecoat gift with Evergreen. Shade with Licorice. Highlight with Evergreen + Taffy.
2. Paint ribbon on gift with Light Red Oxide. Shade with Burnt Carmine. Highlight with Red Light.
3. Paint top section of ball with Barn Wood. Shade with Payne's Gray + Burnt Umber. Highlight with Taffy.
4. Paint stripes on ball with Light Red Oxide. Shade with Burnt Carmine. Highlight with Red Light.
5. Paint lower section of ball with Navy Blue. Shade with Licorice. Highlight with Navy Blue + Taffy.
6. Basecoat bag with Nutmeg. Shade with Burnt Umber. Highlight with Nutmeg + Taffy.

Ornament Background:
1. Basecoat with Light Red Oxide, then add a coat of Lipstick Red. Shade with Burnt Carmine. Highlight with Red Light.
2. Paint strokework with Pure Gold.

Gold Bands & Top of Ornament:
1. Basecoat with English Mustard. Shade with Nutmeg, then Burnt Umber. Highlight with Yellow Light.
2. Paint linework with Yellow Light. Highlight the linework in the middles of the sections with Yellow Light + Taffy.
3. Paint some dots with Yellow Light, others with Pure Gold. Let dry.

4 Finish

1. Make holes in top and bottom of ornament with pushpin. Insert screw eyes.
2. Apply varnish. Let dry.
3. Attach bell to bottom. ❏

Santa Ornament Worksheet

Fig. 1 – Basecoats applied.

Fig. 2 – Shading applied.

Fig. 3 – Highlighting applied.

Fig. 4 – Details added.

Elegant Rose Vest

painted by Judi Krause

*Fabric Painting can allow you to show off your painting in a different way-by wearing your art. This romantic vest was published in **Rose WorkBook** by Plaid Enterprises Inc. in 1996.*

Judi is a designer and teacher of decorative painting. She has been sharing her enthusiasm, skills and ideas with others for over 25 years. A keen and sensitive eye for detail and color and the ability to combine several art forms are evident in Judi's work and characteristic of her style.

Judi has been known for her exquisite and feminine Victorian style of painting. Her work is always recognizable by it's soft colors, roses, and lace elements. The photo at the bottom right are projects from her book, **Timeless Treasures** published in 1988. Even after 13 years the classic style of the art keeps the project designs desirable — truly timeless treasures.

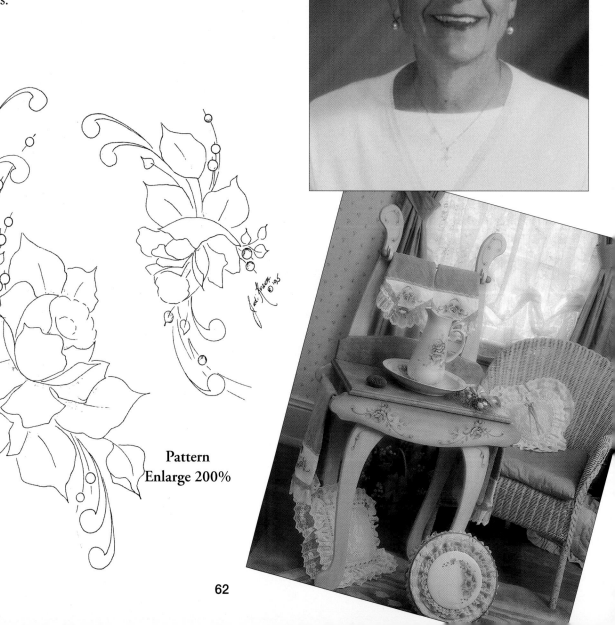

**Pattern
Enlarge 200%**

Elegant Roses Vest

by Judi Krause

1 Gather These Supplies

FolkArt® Acrylic Colors:
Buttercrunch #737
Rose Pink #632
Emerald Isle #647
Sky Blue #465
Raspberry Sherbet #966
Inca Gold Metallic #676

FolkArt® Artists' Pigments:
Titanium White #480
Sap Green #458
Burnt Carmine #686

Painting Surface:
Off White Faille Vest

Other Supplies:
Fashion® Fabric Paint: Gold Glitter
Fabric Flat Brushes: #2, #4, #6, #8, #10
Angular Shading Brush: 1/4"
FolkArt® Textile Medium
FolkArt® Thickener
2 yds. Ecru Lace, 1-1/2" wide
15 white pearls
1 Yd. Gold Metallic Ribbon, 3/8" wide
1 double ivory ribbon rose
Ivory Thread
Shirt Board OR cardboard and plastic wrap
Pink Chalk
Masking Tape
Plastic Kitchen Trash Bag OR plastic Wrap
2 pressing cloths
White Vinegar
Iron and Ironing Board
Wax Paper

2 Preparation

1. When working on washable fabric, pre-wash and dry fabric to remove sizing.
2. Place plastic-wrap covered cardboard or shirt board under front of vest.
3. Trace design on tracing paper. Re-trace design on back of tracing paper with pink chalk.
4. Position traced pattern on fabric. Rub your thumbnail or a stylus over the traced pattern so chalked design transfers to fabric. Remove tracing paper.
5. To keep your vest clean and to keep paint from getting on unwanted areas, slip a plastic bag over the vest and shirt board and secure with tape or clothespins. Carefully cut or tear away bag from the area you are going to paint.

3 Paint the Design

General Techniques

1. Before Painting, mix two parts paint with one part Textile Medium. This alters the paint's chemistry, making it flexible and permanent on fabric. On washable fabrics, paints that are properly mixed and heat set are washable.
2. Because fabrics vary in texture and absorbency, test paint a scrap of fabric, if possible. This gives you a feel for how the fabric reacts to paint and moisture, and can prevent unwanted or uncontrollable bleeding.
3. **For a Bold Look,** apply paint mixed with Textile Medium to dry fabric.
For a soft look, use a wet on wet technique: Dip brush in Textile Medium. Blot on paper towel. Brush sections of design just inside the pattern boundaries. While fabric is moist, shade sections with lightest color value, using a sideloaded flat brush. Using a stiff bristle brush, scrub out the color, creating values dark to medium to light. Then highlight. (highlight areas will be the natural color of the fabric showing through.) Gradually strengthen dark areas, using corner loaded brush and deeper tones.
4. Sharpen edges and refine with linework to add more detail. Allow sections to dry. Add color as desired, using a drier consistency of paint. Stems and veins can be applied with the chisel edge of a flat brush or the tip of a short liner brush, almost skimming the paint over the surface of the fabric. If unwanted bleeding should occur, You may be able to camouflage the bleed area by mixing a color that matches the background.

Understand the Form and Parts of the Rose

Look at the pattern and mentally eliminate all the individual parts and see only the overall shape. Can you see a circle or a sphere? This is the line upon which we will build.

1. Draw a circle and place a dot in the center. This is the point from which all points radiate and join together to become one, the stem and the petals, even when they don't visibly connect. In most designs, the center of the rose is not dead center, but offset; a flower is more appealing when viewed above or below eye level instead of straight on.
2. Number your circle like the face of a clock. This helps when placing petals. In the beginning, the bloom appears as a tightly clasped bud. As the petals unfurl, they open up, drop down, and increase the overall size of the sphere, creating a number of circles within a circle. The main bloom of the rose is like a sphere-shaped cup sitting on a circular saucer (the lower petals). The cup has an inside and an outside. As the rose opens, individual petals become more visible and a layered pattern appears. Petals are light on all outer edges, medium value in the middle, and darker against an overlapping petal or where they connect to the body of the rose. The end of the petals slide or tuck gracefully into the edges of the cup. Construct the rose in three parts: the lower petals or saucer, the inside cup, and the outside cup or front bowl.
3. **Construction of the Lower Petals:** Begin by painting the lower layer first. Continue with successive layers, ending with the top layer of petals. Place lower petals between 3 o'clock and 6 o'clock on the right half of the flower and between 6 o'clock and 10 o'clock on the left side. End side petal strokes by sliding the end of the petal into the edge of the cup at 6 o'clock.
4. **Construction of Inside Cup:** Think of the inside as a deep hole. Curve petals like a frown. The back outside edge petals are choppy, wider strokes, while those approaching the center are smaller, tighter strokes.
5. **Construction of Outside Cup or Front Bowl:** Although we view the rose from one side and only see the petals on the side that's facing us, the petals do continue around the flower. The first strokes on the right and left sides must appear to connect to the inside cup of the rose. Some may fall away, as if bursting open.

Leaves:

The leaves closest to the roses are stronger in value, progressively getting lighter as you move away from the focal point of the design. Outermost leaves should almost fade away into the background. Each leaf should contain three values of color and accent colors corresponding to other colors in the piece.

Leaf Mixes:

#1 (Light value = cream)- Buttercrunch + Titanium White
#2 (medium value = light green)- Sky Blue + Sap Green
#3 (dark value = dark green)- Emerald Isle + touch of Burnt Carmine
Moisten leaf areas with Thickener before painting.

Leaf Technique:

1. Using #10 flat brush, tint tip of leaf to stem with #1 mix. Scrub into fabric. Rinse and dry brush.
2. Light outline edges and stem end with #2 mix. Blend color toward center vein, using #10 flat. Tint stem end, under roses, and down dark half of leaf with #2 mix. Blend color with #10 flat brush and ease down the dark side of center vein, creating color variations from dark to medium to light. (This creates streaks-the impressions of side veins.)
3. Deepen color in shaded areas and on dark side of center vein with touch of Emerald Green + Burnt Carmine.
4. Highlight opposite side of vein with Titanium White + Buttercrunch, using a clean flat brush.
5. Corner load #4 flat brush with Raspberry Sherbet. Tint occasionally on outside edges of leaf. Let dry.
6. Blush leaves in highlight areas with hint of Inca Gold. Let dry.
7. Partially outline tip ends of leaves, edges, and center veins with fine lines of Gold Glitter paint, squeezing paint directly from the tube.
8. Paint tiny leaves with corner loaded #2 flat brush and Sky Blue. Blush with Inca Gold.
9. Paint tendrils and stems with Sky Blue + Emerald Isle + Burnt Carmine, using chisel edge of #2 flat brush.

Roses:

Our goal is to paint soft, delicate roses. Paint is used sparingly. Think of the rose as four basic areas, and work in this order: inside the cup, front of the cup, base petals, and turned petals. Start each area by moistening with Thickener. Working wet paint onto moistened fabric makes blending easier, extends the drying time of the paint, and makes the colors softer.

You can vary the color of the roses by varying the amount of color. For soft, pastel roses, allow light to medium values to dominate and keep shading minimal. For deeper toned roses, make the shading color more prominent.

Rose Color Mixes:

#1 (light value = warm white)-Titanium White + Buttercrunch
#2 (medium value = soft rose)- Rose Pink + Raspberry Sherbet
#3 (dark value)-Burnt Carmine, sparingly, then Burnt Carmine + a dot of Emerald Isle

INSIDE THE CUP:

1. Using the #4 flat brush, tint from outside edges toward center with #1 mix. Blend into fabric with small scrubby brush.
2. Sideload #2 flat brush with #2 mix. Shade from bottom up and blend with curve of outside top edge.
3. Using corner loaded #2 flat brush with #3 mix, strengthen shading at bottom center.
4. Corner load brush with #1 mix. Stroke in two or three rows of petals, starting with outermost row. Wipe brush dry and soften lower edge of petals. Leave a line of color separating each row of petals.

CUPS OF ROSES, PART 1:

5. With #8 or#10 flat brush, tint with #1 mix, starting at top edge and working to bottom.
6. Tint from bottom up with #2 mix. *Notice the contours. You will be blending smile shaped strokes following the curve and contour of the base of the cup.*
7. Establish depth by shading each petal and between petals, using corner loaded #4 flat brush with #3 mix. Clean brush and wipe dry.
8. Highlight top edge of each petal, using corner loaded #4 flat and #1 mix.

FLOWER PETALS:

Treat each petal individually

9. Tint front outer edge with #1 mix. Scrub into fabric. Wipe brush dry.
10. Using corner laded #4 or#6 flat brush, tint overlapping petal with #2 mix, blending color 2/3 way out on each petal. Rinse brush and wipe dry.

CUPS OF ROSES, PART 2:

11. Corner load brush with Titanium White and paint two or three strokes at front of cup, positioning brush with white edge at top of cup. Paint smile shaped strokes around top of front of cup.

BERRIES & SCROLLS:

moisten areas with Thickener before painting.

12. Using #2 flat brush, tint each berry with Titanium White + Inca Gold. Tint scrolls with Inca Gold.
13. Wipe Brush Dry. Corner Load with Burnt Carmine. Shade to contour. Rinse brush. Dry Blend.
14. Highlight light sides of berries with tiny dot or comma stroke of Titanium White.
15. With Gold Glitter paint, outline rounded ends and necks of scrolls. Using clean, dry #2 flat brush, pull glitter into rounded ends of scrolls. Let dry.

4 Finish

Heat Set:

1. Remove vest from protective plastic bag and shirt board. Place dry painted fabric, right side up, on a pressing cloth on ironing board. Dampen another cloth with white vinegar. Wring out excess. Place cloth over painted design. Top with wax paper. With warm iron, press and lift on wax paper. Remove wax paper and vinegar pressing clot. Turn fabric over. Press on wrong side.

Trim:

1. Pin lace trim around outside front edges of neckline, folding under raw edges to give the look of lapels.
2. Pin lace to underside down front of vest, pleating lace every 2-3". Fold edges under.
3. Stitch in place.
4. Pin metallic ribbon to vest, using photograph as guide, pinching-turning-twisting-folding ribbon. Stitch in place.
5. Sew pearls to vest, using photograph as a guide for placement. Sew ribbon roses at center front. ❏

ELEGANT ROSES VEST

Worksheet

Leaves

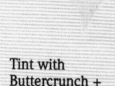 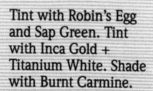 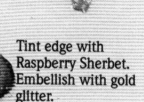

Tint with Buttercrunch + Titanium White.

Tint with Robin's Egg and Sap Green. Tint with Inca Gold + Titanium White. Shade with Burnt Carmine.

Shade with Emerald Isle and Burnt Carmine.

Tint edge with Raspberry Sherbet. Embellish with gold glitter.

Rose—Inside Cup

 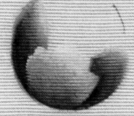

Tint with Buttercrunch + Titanium White. Blush with Raspberry Sherbet + Rose Pink.

Shade with Burnt Carmine + touch of Emerald Isle. Stroke petals with Titanium White + Buttercrunch.

Highlight with Titanium White. Embellish with gold glitter.

Rose—Front of Cup

Tint with Buttercrunch + Titanium White. Blush with Rose Pink + Raspberry Sherbet.

Shade with Burnt Carmine. Then shade with Burnt Carmine + Emerald Isle.

Highlight top edges with Titanium White + Buttercrunch.

Rose—Lower Petals

Tint with Buttercrunch. Blush with Rose Pink + Raspberry Sherbet.

Shade with Burnt Carmine. Then shade with Burnt Carmine and Emerald Isle.

Highlight with Titanium White + Buttercrunch. Paint additional petal strokes around top and front of cup.

See Project Instructions on page 71

Black-Eyed Susan Worksheet

Step 3:
Apply a tiny amount of Burnt Sienna + Burnt Umber wash where petals touch centers. Allow to dry. Paint remaining petals the same way.

Stems

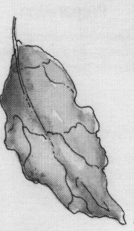

Step 1:
Apply Clover wash to entire stem. Touch down a wash of Thicket along the outside edges and under petals.

Step 2:
Apply tiny amounts of Southern Pine wash to some outside edges of main stem areas to darken.

Step 2:
Apply Burnt Sienna + Burnt Umber wash to dark areas and tips of petals.

Leaves

Step 1: Apply a wash of Clover. Apply wash of Thicket to dark areas and along some outside edges.

Step 2:
Wet some outside areas and apply Burnt Sienna wash.

Flower Petals

Step 1:
Apply a wash of Tangerine, touching down color and allowing it to spread.

Flower Centers

Step 1:
Apply Antique Gold wash. While center is **just** damp, apply Burnt Sienna wash to outside edges and in left curve of hollow.

Step 2:
Apply Burnt Umber wash over Burnt Sienna, but **don't** cover all the Burnt Sienna.

67

Black Eyed Susan   painted by Dolores Lennon

*Since the 16th century, botanical illustrations have tried to capture nature's beauty on paper. Dolores shows you how to paint this beautiful wildflower with just one brush and pen and ink. This project was first published in **Wildflowers**.*

Dolores Lennon, M.D.A. is a certified Master Decorative Artist of the Society of Decorative Painters. Her twelfth decorative painting book is scheduled to be released in late 2001. Writing and developing instructional books provides an outlet for what Dolores loves most – teaching.

Dolores' love of and experience in gardening has a profound effect on her art. She is a Master Gardener and constantly learning.

In 1991 her only entry into fine art won first place in the intermediate/advanced watercolor category at the Indianapolis Art League. The subject was a botanical watercolor of "Pelargonium," commonly known as "Geranium."

Rudbeckia hirta
© 1996
Dolores Lennon

Pattern
Enlarge 200%
for actual size

Rudbeckia hirta

©1996

Dolores Lennon's Tips and Techniques

Inking the Design

I am not a "professional" inker. However, I am neat and somewhat precise. In these projects, you must be neat. Once the design has been carefully transferred to the watercolor paper, you are ready to ink unless otherwise stated.

1. Place a folded clean paper towel under your inking hand to prevent any oil from your skin from getting on the paper. It also helps to keep your paper clean.

2. Turn on some soft music and follow the traced design. If you have a "shaky hand," this book is for you. Mother Nature rarely produces a flower petal or leaf with a perfect architectural edge. Go with it. A few more waves or ripples will only enhance the drawing.

Painting the Design

Set up your palette. Squeeze out pea-size amounts of paint onto the waxed palette as you need them. (For example, put out the colors for the flower petals and paint the petals. Then put out colors for the leaves, paint the leaves, and so on. This will help save paint as the problem of acrylic paints drying out will not occur.) Label the colors on the palette with a ballpoint pen, if necessary.

Fill two containers with clean water. One is for rinsing your brush and the other is for use on the palette. You must have one container of clean water at all times for making "washes" of paint. You need only minute amounts of paint pigment in washes. See "Painting Terms" for how to create washes.

Painting Terms

Wash: Simply drop some clean water from your brush onto the palette next to the color being used. Pull out some paint with the tip of the brush and mix with the water. Rinse out the brush and blot it on a paper towel. Now pick up the "wash" of color on your brush. Also use this method when thinned paint is specified.

Dampen: Pick up clean water with the brush and blot on a clean paper towel. "Paint" the designated area with clean water.

Dab or **Touch:** Pick up a wash of the color indicated and touch the tip of the brush to a *damp* area. Allow to spread.

Leaving White Areas: When applying the first wash throughout the design, do not attempt to fill in the whole area with color. Leaving some white, unpainted areas will greatly enhance the natural effect. The white areas will look like highlights.

Shadow Areas: These areas are generally underneath or behind and between petals and leaves.

Soften: Apply a wash of color. Rinse the brush quickly and blot on a paper towel. Pat the color gently. This will soften the color's edge. Work quickly when softening.

Streaking This is done with a minimal amount of color wash and the *very tip* of your brush. Barely make contact with the surface of the paper as you follow the diagrams and/or painting worksheets.

Thinned: See "Wash."

Travel: After touching down a color wash on a damp area, allow it to spread of its own accord.

Tuck: This term refers to placement of a dark value in a *tiny* shadow area. Use the softening technique. ❏

Black-Eyed Susan

By Dolores Lennon

1 Gather These Supplies

FolkArt® Acrylic Colors:
Tangerine #627
Clover #923
Old Ivy #927
Thicket #924
Copper Metallic #664
English Mustard #959

FolkArt® Artists' Pigments:
Yellow Light #918
Burnt Sienna #943
Burnt Umber #462

Painting Surface:
Watercolor Paper, 14" x19"

Other Supplies:
Round Sable Brush #8
A Rapidoliner, size .25 pen made by
    Koh-I-Noor

2 Preparation

1. Trace design and transfer to paper
2. Carefully ink the design.

3 Paint The Design

Order of Painting:
1. Flower Petals
2. Flower Centers
3. Leaves
4. Stems

Flower Petals:
1. Make washes of Tangerine, Yellow Light, and Copper. Wet every other petal, Leaving some dry areas in the centers of petals. (These are the high-lights-they will stay white.) Apply a wash of Tangerine, touching down color and allowing it to spread. Quickly add a wash of Yellow Light, then a wash of Copper. Allow to dry.
2. Make a wash of Burnt Sienna + Burnt Umber. Wet dark areas with water. Apply Burnt Sienna + Burnt Umber wash to dark areas and tips of petals.
3. While petals are still damp, apply a tiny amount of Burnt Sienna + Burnt Umber wash where petals touch centers. Allow to dry.
4. Paint remaining petals the same way.

Flower Centers:
1. Make washes of English Mustard and Burnt Sienna. Wet center. Apply English Mustard wash. While center is **just** damp, apply Burnt Sienna wash to outside edges and in left curve of hollow. Allow to dry.
2. Make a wash of Burnt Umber. Wet dark areas. Apply Burnt Umber wash over Burnt Sienna, but **don't** cover all the Burnt Sienna. Keep the Burnt Umber wash light around outside edges and in the hollow.

Leaves:
1. Make washes of Clover, Thicket, and Old Ivy. Wet leaf. Apply a wash of Clover. Apply wash of Thicket to dark areas and along some outside edges. Tuck a small amount of Old Ivy very tightly in shadow areas.
2. Make a wash of Burnt Sienna. Wet some outside areas and apply Burnt Sienna wash. See "Black-Eyed Susan Worksheet."

Stems:
1. Apply Clover wash to entire stem. Using the tip of the brush, touch down a wash of Thicket along the outside edges and under petals.
2. Apply tiny amounts of Old Ivy wash to some outside edges of main stem areas to darken. Allow to dry. ❏

4 Finish

Add additional inking if needed. ❏

Black Eyed Susan Value Placement Diagram

Key:

= dark

Smilin' Jack Pumpkin

painted by Cindy Mann

*This delightful handmade greeting card is from **Heartfelt Greetings**.
This book was Cindy's 7th book with Plaid Enterprises, Inc.*

In 1995 Cindy's friend, Diane Capoccia, urged her to put her wonderful designs into a book form. Previous to that she was attending shows and selling her designs in pattern packets. So in 1996 she published her first book with Plaid, entitled, *The Checkerboard Collections.*

Cindy attends the Hoot Convention in Columbus each year. She also occasionally writes magazine articles and designs pattern packets. In addition, Cindy designs home decor items and a Christmas line for a company that offers reproduced pieces.

Cindy recently moved into a historical and much smaller home in Germantown, Ohio. As a result, she's lucky to have her daughter, son-in-law, and grandson living right next door. Cindy's other daughter is attending college at Ohio State University. Cindy says, "What with designing, unpacking, redecorating, coordinating with my college student, and fitting in time to play with Jacob, my grandson, my days are indeed full!"

You can contact Cindy at:
937-855-6006 OR
www.cindymann.com
info@cindymann.com (for questions and comments)
orders@cindymann.com (to place orders)

*This photo is a project from Cindy's first book published by Plaid, **The Checkerboard Collection**.*

Smilin' Jack Card with Fashion Pin

∽∞∽

By Cindy Mann

1 Gather These Supplies

FolkArt® Acrylic Colors:
Acorn Brown #941
Barnyard Red #611
Buttercup #905
Charcoal Grey #613
Clay Bisque #601
Country Twill #602
Huckleberry #745
Italian Sage #467
Maple Syrup #945
Sunflower #432
Terra Cotta #433

FolkArt® Artists' Pigments:
Burnt Carmine #686
Burnt Umber #462
Green Umber #471
Pure Black #479
Raw Sienna #452
Warm White #649

Painting Surface:
Watercolor paper, #140 cold press
White envelope to fit 5" x 7" card (use bubble wrap envelope if including the pin)
Scarecrow wood cutout (cut by pattern from 1/8" wood)

Other Supplies:
FolkArt® Antiquing Medium: Woodn' Bucket Brown #817
Black Zig permanent ink pen, size #005
Art deckle ruler
Toothbrush
Craft knife
Bar pin back, 1"
Raffia
FolkArt® Antiquing Medium: Woodn' Bucket Brown #817
FolkArt® ClearCote™ Matte Acrylic Sealer #789
FolkArt® Artist Varnish, satin finish #887
Thick white craft glue
Hot glue gun and glue sticks

2 Preparation

1. Sand wood cutout smooth and wipe away dust.
2. Cut watercolor paper to 7" x 10-1/2".

Tear one 7" edge using art deckle ruler. This will be open edge of card front. Measure and mark paper at center, then fold and crease for a 7" x 10" card with side fold.
3. Spray a light coat of matte acrylic sealer on lower left corner of envelope where design will be.
4. Transfer designs to card, wood cutout, and lower left front corner of envelope. Do not transfer any interior details. (NOTE: If you do not wish to make the pin, you can transfer the scarecrow pattern directly to the card.)

3 Paint the Design

Pumpkin (On Card & Envelope):
Refer to "Smilin' Jack" Pumpkin Worksheet.
1. Basecoat eyes and nose of pumpkin on card with Buttercup. Shade with Raw Sienna. Basecoat the visible thickness of pumpkin in these areas with Warm White. Shade these areas with Burnt Umber.
2. Paint eyes and nose of pumpkin on envelope with Pure Black.
3. Basecoat lips with Barnyard Red. Shade lips on card with Burnt Carmine.
4. Basecoat teeth with Warm White. Shade corners with very diluted Pure Black.
5. Basecoat the pumpkin with Terra Cotta and shade with Huckleberry.
6. Basecoat stem of pumpkin on envelope with Italian Sage. Shade with Green Umber.

Moon & Stars:
1. Basecoat moon with Sunflower. Shade with Raw Sienna.
2. Basecoat stars with Buttercup. Shade with Raw Sienna.

Checkerboard Area:
1. Basecoat gold squares with Buttercup. Shade with Raw Sienna.
2. Basecoat black checkerboard squares with Charcoal Grey. Shade with Pure Black.

Background:
Float Burnt Umber around outer edges of card and around lower left corner of envelope.

Scarecrow (Wood Cutout:)
1. Basecoat pumpkin head with Terra Cotta. Shade with Huckleberry.
2. Basecoat head-pumpkin stem with Italian Sage. Shade with Green Umber.
3. Paint eyes and nose with Pure Black.
4. Basecoat collar and gloves with Clay Bisque. Shade with Burnt Umber.
5. Basecoat overalls with Acorn Brown. Shade with Maple Syrup.
6. Basecoat heart patch with Barnyard Red. Shade with Burnt Carmine.
7. Basecoat star patch with Sunflower. Shade with Raw Sienna.
8. Basecoat sleeves with Sunflower. Shade with Raw Sienna. Paint stripes with Green Umber.
9. Basecoat shoes with Country Twill. Shade with Burnt Umber.

4 Finish

1. Brush wood cutout with a light even coat of slightly diluted waterbase varnish. Let dry completely.
2. Brush a light coat of antiquing diluted 50/50 with water on wood cutout. Use antiquing to stain sides and back of wood.
3. When completely dry, draw linework details and outlining on wood cutout, card, and envelope with the black pen.
4. Spatter all surfaces with Burnt Umber, using the toothbrush.
5. Hot-glue pin back to backside of wood.
6. Cut thin strips of raffia into 6" lengths. Tie in center to hold together. Glue raffia in place to card with thick white craft glue (refer to photo of project for placement).
7. Place wood cutout in position on card design and mark on card the placement of pin's position. Cut two 1/4" vertical slits in card from with craft knife on these markings. Make them close enough together to allow pin bar to side through card and fasten easily.
8. Pin card in place on card front. ❏

Smilin'Jack Card & Pin Pattern

By Cindy Mann

Card & Wood Cutout Design
Cut pumpkin scarecrow woodcut from 1/8" wood.

**Envelope
Design**

Actual size

Pumpkin Painting Worksheet

1. Basecoat:
Pumpkin – Terra Cotta.
Eyes, nose – Buttercup.
Thickness of pumpkin in eyes, nose – Warm White
Lips – Barnyard Red
Teeth – Warm White

2. Shade:
Pumpkin – Huckleberry
Eyes, nose – Raw Sienna
Thickness of pumpkin in eyes, nose – Burnt Umber
Lips – Burnt Carmine
Teeth – very diluted (80/20) Pure Black

3. Draw details and outlining with black permanent pen. Spatter surfaces – Pure Black

Wintertime Pals Sled Pattern

by Dianna Marcum

Instructions on page 80

Enlarge 155%
for actual size

Wintertime Pals

painted by Dianna Marcum

*What a way to ride! The sled is a nice painting surface. Use it as
a tabletop decoration, place it under your tree, or hang it on the wall.
The nice flat surface allows lots of space for showing off your painting.
This cute holiday offering is from **Penguins & Polar Bears**.*

Dianna Marcum lives with her husband Randy on a farm in rural Missouri. Surrounded by the countryside and an ever-growing assortment of pets, she creates whimsical characters that have found their way into other mediums, such as fabrics, painting books, rubber stamps, and buttons. She has authored the popular **Bless Your Heart** series of painting books.

Dianna's designs will always bring a smile to your face. They are cheerful and sometimes whimsical, and the clear colors add brightness to your painting. ❑

Wintertime Pals
Decorative Sled

Wintertime Pals Sled

∞

By Dianna Marcum

1 Gather These Supplies:

FolkArt® Acrylic Colors:
Licorice #938
Honeycomb #942
Real Brown #231
English Mustard #959
Teal #405
Copper (Metallic) #664
Winter White #429
Charcoal Gray #613
Parchment #450
Thicket #924
Green #408
Wrought Iron #925
Heartland Blue #608
Buttercrunch #737
Navy Blue #403
Cardinal Red #414
Medium Gray #425

FolkArt® Artists' Pigments:
Yellow Light #918
Napthol Crimson #435
Indian Blue #236

Project Surface:
Wooden sled with metal runners, wood surface 7" x 13"

2 Preparation

1. Remove runners from sled.
2. Prepare wood, following instructions in Tips & Techniques section.
3. Trace and transfer pattern.

3 Paint the Design:

Sky:
1. Base with Indian Blue.
2. Dry brush with Teal, then with Teal + Winter White.
3. Use a large flat brush to float Navy Blue next to penguin and polar bear outlines.

Snow:
1. Base with Parchment.
2. Load a large, dry brush with Winter White and slip-slap paint, using a horizontal motion, across the snow. Don't cover all of the background.
3. Float Medium Gray under polar bear's feet. Float Teal in the same areas and below. See photo for color placement.

Penguin:
1. Base light body areas with Parchment.
2. Shade with Charcoal Gray.
3. Color tummies and cheeks with Copper.
4. Base beaks and feet with English Mustard. Shade with Honeycomb, then with Yellow Light. Add additional shading with Real Brown.
5. Base dark body areas with Licorice. Highlight with Teal.
6. Dot eyes and paint brows with Licorice.
7. Add Parchment highlights to eyes and cheeks.

Penguin's Cap:
1. Paint fur trim with Parchment.
2. Paint cap with Promenade, then Cardinal Red. (This gives better coverage and a bit brighter color.)
3. Shade with Navy Blue.
4. Using a scruffy brush, pounce Winter White on fur trim. Float with Charcoal Gray to shade, then with Teal.
5. Mix Real Brown + a touch of Licorice. Outline and add squiggly details.

Penguin's Scarf:
1. Paint with Promenade, then Cardinal Red.
2. Paint light stripes with Parchment. Paint thin stripes with Green.
3. Shade with Napthol Crimson, then Navy Blue.

Polar Bear:
1. Base with Parchment.
2. Use a scruffy brush to pounce on Parchment + Winter White to make fur. Pick up a little more Winter White and pounce in light areas: muzzle, front ear, legs closest to you, rump.
3. Use a large flat brush to float Charcoal Gray shading. Then float with Buttercrunch, coming out further, and along the back leg and rump to give the bear a creamy color. Add darkest shading with Medium Gray.
4. Thin Medium Gray and paint a squiggly outline with a liner brush.
5. Blush cheek and inside ear with Copper.
6. Paint eyes, brows, and nose with Licorice. Highlight eyes and nose with Parchment.

Bells:
1. Paint collar and rein with Thicket. Shade with Licorice. Highlight with Green.
2. Paint bells with English Mustard. Shade with Honeycomb, then with Napthol Crimson. Highlight with Winter White.
3. Outline and add detail with Real Brown + Licorice.

Snowflakes:
1. Paint lines for snowflakes with thinned Parchment.
2. Add dots of Parchment to ends of snowflakes and for snow. Let dry.

4 Finish

1. Paint edges and back of sled with Promenade, then with Cardinal Red. Let dry.
2. Varnish, following instructions in Tips & Techniques section.
3. Replace runners. ❏

Penguin Painting Worksheet

ILLUSTRATION ONE:

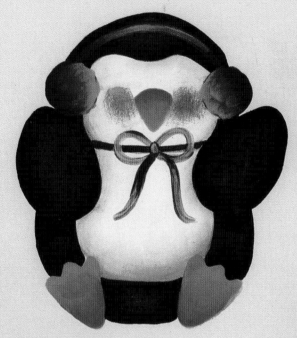

ILLUSTRATION TWO:

ILLUSTRATION THREE:

SKY:

1. Base with Heartland Blue.
2. Dry brush with Teal, then Teal + Tapioca to add interest.
3. Float Navy Blue to shade.
4. Add snowflakes with thinned Tapioca. Add accents and random dots with Tapioca.

Polar Bear Painting Worksheet

ILLUSTRATION ONE:

ILLUSTRATION TWO:

ILLUSTRATION THREE:

ILLUSTRATION FOUR:

Cat Lover's Welcome Sign Pattern

By Helen Nicholson

See Instructions on page 85

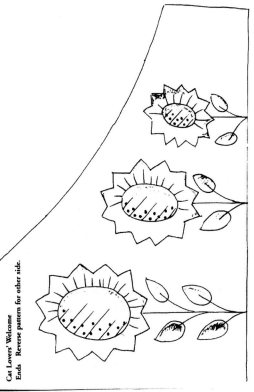

Cat Lovers' Welcome
Ends Reverse pattern for other side.

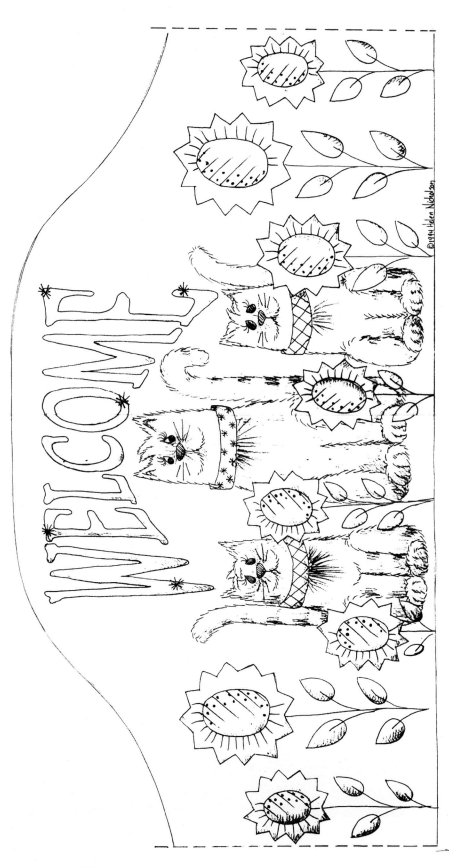

**Enlarge
200%
for
actual
size**

Cat Lovers' Welcome

painted by Helen Nicholson

*These charming painted projects for the beginning painter were published in **Kitties In The Garden** by Plaid Enterprises in 1995. The delightful colors and whimsical designs are a good example of this creative artists' style.*

Helen Nicholson has painted for over 26 years as a fine artist, craft manufacturer, and now designer and author. She creates "How-To" craft projects for the home painter in leading craft magazines nationwide and has authored several painting books and designed iron-on transfers for *Plaid Enterprises, Inc.* Between writing books and magazine articles and designing projects and iron-ons, Helen spends her time working on artistic projects for children with special needs.

You may contact this artist at:
Helen Nicholson Designs
P.O. Box 232
Lebanon, GA 30146

Cat Lovers' Welcome

By Helen Nicholson

1 Gather These Supplies

FolkArt® Acrylic Colors:

Wicker White #901	Thicket #924
Poppy Red 630	Buttercream #614
Wrought Iron #925	Tangerine #627
Real Brown #231	Lipstick Red #437
Honeycomb #942	Charcoal Gray #613
Dapple Gray #937	Thunder Blue #609
Licorice #938	Kelly Green #407

FolkArt® Artists' Pigments:
Indian Blue #236
Yellow Light #918

Painting Surface:
Plaque cut from 1" pine; according to
   pattern

Brushes:
Liner Brush #1
Round Brush #3, #5
Flat Brush #4, #6, #8, #10
Old toothbrush
Sponge Brush 1"

Other Supplies:
Matte Acrylic Sealer
FolkArt® Waterbase Varnish
Fine Sandpaper
Tack Cloth
Stylus
Graph paper

2 Preparation

1. Apply a coat of Minwax "Early American" stain. Allow to soak in a few minutes, then wipe off excess stain with a rag. Allow to dry for several hours or overnight. When dry seal the wood with FolkArt® Waterbase Varnish and let dry. Sand well. Wipe away sanding dust with a slightly damp rag or tack cloth.
2. Transfer lettering and outline of kitties using a stylus and graph paper.
3. Basecoat each kitty, referring to base colors in painting steps below. Add a second coat to smooth out color and provide a good surface for shading.
4. Float Real Brown around kitties and lettering on background. Repeat to deepen shading.

3 Paint the Design

Black Kitty:
Base Color: Licorice
1. Sideload a brush with Dapple Gray and add fur details. When dry, highlight with a float of Wicker White. Add additional fur details with Wicker White.
2. Basecoat collar with Poppy Red. Shade with Lipstick Red. Highlight with Tangerine. Add stars and Wicker White.

Gray Kitty:
Base Color: Dapple Gray
1. Sideload a flat brush with Licorice and stipple fur. Rinse brush and repeat with Charcoal Gray. Let dry completely. Float Licorice along feet, legs, bottom of tail, under head, bottom of body and alongside rear haunch.
2. Highlight face, feet, legs, and tail with a float of Wicker White. When dry, add fine lines of Wicker White to edges of body, legs, feet, tail, chin, and on chest to resemble fur.
3. Basecoat collar with Indian Blue. Shade with Thunder Blue. Highlight with Wicker White. When dry, add lines of Wicker White.

Brown Kitty:
Base Color: Nutmeg
1. Stipple fur with thinned Real Brown. When dry, shade first with Real Brown, then with Licorice. Let dry.
2. Highlight face, tail, feet, and face.
3. Basecoat collar with Indian Blue. Shade with Thunder Blue. Highlight with Wicker White. When dry, add lines of Wicker White.

All Kitties:
1. Basecoat eyes and noses with Licorice. Highlight with a float of Wicker White. Add Wicker White dots for highlight.
2. Blush ears and cheeks with a float of Poppy Red.

Lettering:
Base Color: Licorice
1. Highlight lettering with a float of Dapple Gray along right side of each letter. Highlight further by floating Wicker White lightly along upper right of each letter.
2. Add stars here and there to letters.

Flowers:
1. Yellow Flowers: Base petal area with Yellow Light. Shade with Honeycomb. Highlight with Wicker White. Base flower center with Honeycomb. Shade with Real Brown. When dry, paint linework on petals with Honeycomb and linework on center with Wicker White.
2. White Flowers: Base petal area with Buttercream. Shade with Yellow Light, then shade deeper with Honeycomb. Base flower centers with Real Brown and shade with Licorice. When dry, paint linework on petals with Real Brown and on centers with Wicker White.
3. Red Flowers: Base petal area with Tangerine. Shade with Poppy Red. Base flower center with Buttercream. Shade with Honeycomb. When dry, paint linework with Real Brown.
4. Stems: Base with Real Brown. Shade with Licorice.
5. Leaves: Base with Kelly Green. Shade with Thicket. Highlight with Yellow Light.

Finishing Touches:
1. Add fur details, eyelashes, and whiskers on each cat with thinned Wicker White.
2. Speckle sign first with Wicker White, then with Real Brown. Let dry completely.

4 Finish

1. Mist entire piece with Matte Sealer. Let dry.
2. Apply three or four coats of FolkArt® Waterbase Varnish. This project is for limited use in the garden. Recoat with water base varnish every few months to keep painting fresh. ❏

Yellow Roses Box

painted by Judy Nutter

*This lovely wooden box appeared in **The Rose WorkBook** in
1996 published by Plaid Enterprises, Inc.
It is a classic design that has become a favorite by all.*

Judi Nutter has been designing and teaching decorative art for more than twenty five years. An accomplished artist in both oil and acrylics, she is a member of the National Society of Decorative Painters. Judy passed the Society's certification program in 1978 and a portion of the master program in 1979.

When not traveling across the U.S. and Canada teaching seminars, Judy enjoys designing projects for her books and being with her family in Lafayette, LA. Judy teaches at many decorative painting mini conventions as well as at the NSDP's National Convention.

**Pattern
Enlarge 120%
for actual size**

YELLOW ROSES BOX

Worksheet

Shadow Leaves
Paint with Aspen Green.

Major Leaves
Base with Basil Green. Shade with Basil Green + Thicket. Line with Thicket.

Branches
Base with Thicket + Burgundy. Highlight with Buttercream.

Fluff in color

1
3
2
4

Shadow leaves washed with Yellow Medium.

1

Wash shadow leaves with Yellow Medium

Highlight leaves with Buttercream.

Under petals

Side petals

Wash leaves with Yellow Light. Tint with Red Orange + Burgundy.

Yellow Roses Box

By Judy Nutter

1 Gather These Supplies

FolkArt® Acrylic Colors:
Basil Green #645
Thicket #924
Buttercream #614
English Mustard #959
Aspen Green #646
Burgundy #957
Dove Grey #708
Buttercup #905

FolkArt® Artists' Pigments:
Yellow Light #918
Red Light #629

Painting Surface:
Round Wooden Box, 10" diameter

Brushes:
Angular Brush 1/2", 3/8"
Shader Brush #14
Liner Brush #1
Flat Brush #20
Flat Shader Brush #8

Other Supplies:
FolkArt® Waterbase Varnish
FolkArt® Extender
Sandpaper
Wood Sealer
Tack Cloth
Sponge

2 Preparation

1. Prepare box for painting. Basecoat top of lid with Dove Grey and side of lid and box base with Aspen Green. Let dry.
2. Thin Dove Grey with a little water. Sponge mixture on sides of box.
3. Trace pattern and transfer to lid.

3 Paint the Design

Background
1. Using #20 flat brush, paint top of lid with Dove Grey + Extender. While still wet, slip-slap Buttercream here and there on the right side of the design.
2. Deepen left side of the design with Aspen Green. Add Aspen Green to the outer right edge of the box lid. Let dry.
3. Paint Buttercream area with a very light was of Yellow Light. Wipe off excess while color is still wet.
4. Trace and transfer pattern to top of lid.

Shadow Leaves:
1. Load #8 Flat Shader with Aspen Green + Extender. Very Loosely, suggest shadow leaves. Use less Extender for leaves under roses so they will be darker. See photograph for color placement.
2. With side loaded #14 flat shader, tuck Thicket + Burgundy in the obvious shadow points under the flowers to deepen the shadow leaves.

Branches:
1. Fill liner brush with Thicket + Burgundy. Pull branches.
2. Flatten liner brush and edge into Buttercream. Apply highlights to right edge of branches.

Larger Rose:
Use angular brushes, choosing the size appropriate for the area.
1. Fluff in Buttercup, in cup portion of flower. While still wet, deepen throat with English Mustard + Red Light.
2. Sideload angular brush with Buttercup + a touch of Buttercream on the long side. Stroke the back petals picking up more Buttercream as the strokes come forward.
3. Sideload again with Buttercup + Buttercream and stroke the front petals, making the strokes lighter as you come forward. Make two disconnected strokes at the front of the rose. These are the lightest strokes.
4. Deepen the throat with a sideloaded float of English Mustard + Red Light. Let dry. Further deepen with burgundy + a touch of Thicket.
5. Deepen in the triangular areas where back and front petals meet with English Mustard + Red Light.
6. Load the angular brush with Buttercup + Buttercream on the long edge and English Mustard + Red Light on the short side. Blend well on the palette to soften colors before stroking in the saucer portion of the rose.
7. Highlight with a sideload of Buttercream on some edges and in the ripple areas. See Worksheet.
8. Deepen shadow points with a sideloaded float of English Mustard + Burgundy.
9. Tint with Red Light + English Mustard.
10. When flowers are complete, wash here and there with Yellow Light to warm them, using a flat brush.
11. Dab Buttercup in center bowl of rose. Highlight with dabs of Buttercream.
12. Soften Outer Edges with a wash of Dove Grey.

Smaller Rose:
1. Paint smaller rose in the same manner, but don't apply quite as much Red Light or such strong highlights. Keep values closer.

Major Leaves:
1. Base leaves with Basil Green.
2. Line with Thicket, creating major and auxiliary veins.
3. Sideload brush with Basil Green + Thicket. Shade outer edges randomly and in dark shadow points.
4. Sideload brush with Buttercream. Highlight on each side of major vein and between auxiliary veins with C-strokes. Stagger some strokes so the center vein is virtually lost. Highlight here and there on edges with Buttercream.
5. Darken some shadow points again with Thicket + Burgundy.
6. Randomly wash highlight area with Yellow Light. Wipe back to lighten highlights while wash is still wet.

Unifying Details:
1. Wash flower petals which touch leaves with Thicket.
2. Wash any areas which appear too bright into the background with Dove Grey.

4 Finish

Varnish protects, and enhances painted surfaces and offers resistance to scratches and water spotting. FolkArt® Waterbase Varnish is easy to use and gives a soft satin finish.
1. Brush a coat of FolkArt® Waterbase Varnish. Let dry. "Sand" by rubbing surface with a piece of brown paper bag. (This acts as a very fine sandpaper.)
2. Apply additional coats of varnish. Let dry and "sand" between coats. Let cure for several days.
3. **Optional:** Apply one coat of a good paste furniture wax and polish.
4. Apply several coats of waterbase Varnish. Let dry between coats. ❑

Country Sideboard painted by *PCM* Studios

*This sideboard is a part of a complete kitchen of wonderful painting techniques. **Creative Home Painting** published by Plaid, showcased these two talented designers.*

*P*hillip C. Myer and Andy B. Jones are business partners in PCM Studios, where they design and create custom painted furniture, accessories, and interiors. They also design unfinished wood lines and products, books, brushes, and videos for the decorative painter.

Phillip and Andy teach seminars on decorative painting and faux finishes at their studios in Atlanta, Georgia as well as across the United States and internationally. They have authored dozens of how-to books including *Creative Paint Finishes for the Home* and *Decorative Paint Finishes for the Home*. Plaid has published a series of their books that combine decorative painting with faux finishes. For more information on their seminars, contact them at:
PCM Studios
731 Highland Avenue, N.E., Suite D
Atlanta, GA 30312
404-222-0348
E-mail: abjpcm@aol.com for more information on their seminars

Pictured:
left – Phillip Myer;
right – Andy Jones

Country Sideboard

By PCM Studios

1 Gather These Supplies for Finishing Sideboard

Durable Colors™:
Damask Blue #53314

Decorator Glaze:
Black #53034
Nantucket Navy #53025
Neutral #53001

FolkArt® Artists' Pigments:
Napthol Crimson #435

Decorator Tools:
Stippler Brush #30128

Painting Surface:
Wooden sideboard, unfinished furniture

Other Supplies:
Sandpaper
Tack rag
White stain-blocking primer
Sponge roller and cover
FolkArt® Artists' Varnish – satin water
    base varnish #885

2 Follow These Instructions

Prepare & Base Paint:
1. Prime the surface with white stain-blocking primer. Apply several coats until opaque. Let dry. Sand surface lightly. Remove sanding dust with tack cloth.
2. Base paint the sideboard with two coats Damask Blue, applying smooth strokes of paint across the entire piece. Sand lightly between coats. Remove sanding dust with tack cloth.

Stipple:
1. To create a deep blue-gray glaze, mix equal amounts Nantucket Navy and Black Decorator Glazes. Pour colors into a small tub and mix with palette knife. Slowly add Neutral Glaze and mix, using two parts of the blue-black glaze mixture to three parts Neutral Glaze.
2. Brush a section of the sideboard about 1' square with the blue-gray glaze (Photo 1). While glaze is wet, pounce surface with the Stippler Brush to develop a soft stippled pattern (Photo 2). Wipe brush on a rag from time to time to remove glaze buildup. Continue with this process, working one section at a time, until the surface of the sideboard is complete. Let dry.
3. To shade the edges of the sideboard, dip the tips of the Stippler Brush in the blue-gray glaze mixture. Pounce the brush bristles on the edges of sideboard. Reload brush as needed. See photos for color placement. Let dry.

Paint Apples:
1. Trace and transfer the apple, leaves, and branch designs to the surfaces. Use white transfer paper and a stylus.
2. Undercoat the entire design with Titanium White. Apply two to three coats to achieve opacity. Let dry.
3. Paint leaves, apples, branches, and tendrils, following instructions for "How to Paint Apples." See Apple Worksheet. Let dry 24 hours.

Finish:
1. Using a script liner brush, paint thin outlines with Napthol Crimson around the top and the front apron. Use photo as a guide for placement. Let dry.
2. Seal and protect with several coats Artist's Varnish. Let dry between coats. ❏

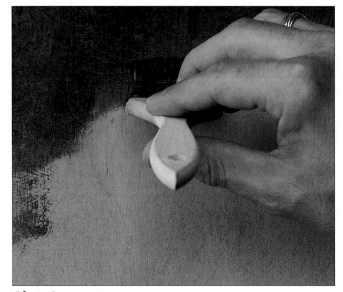

Photo 1

Photo 2

Pattern
Enlarge
145%
for actual
size

How to Paint Apples

By PCM Studios

1 Gather These Supplies for Painting Apples

FolkArt® Artists' Pigments:
Burnt Umber #462
Ice Blue #457
Medium Yellow #455
Napthol Crimson #435
Pure Black #479
Red Light #629
Titanium White #480
True Burgundy #456

Artist's Paint Brushes:
Flat shaders - #8, 12, 16
Script liner - #2

Other Supplies:
FolkArt® Blending Gel Medium #867

2 Instructions for Painting Apples

Leaves:
The leaves are painted with a wet-into-wet technique, working one leaf at a time.

1. Mix a yellow-green color with three parts Medium Yellow + two parts Pure Black.
2. Apply Blending Gel Medium to one leaf.
3. Double load a flat shader with yellow-green mix and Pure Black. Stroke brush on the palette to soften color. Place the dark shading at the base of the leaf or where one leaf goes under another with the Pure Black on the outer edge. (Fig. 5)
4. Establish the center vein of the leaf by stroking the double loaded brush on the left side of the leaf. Wipe brush on a paper towel. Fill in center areas with Yellow Medium. Place yellow-green mixture on top outer edges. (Fig. 5)
5. Stroke to blend colors and break up distinct color divisions from the top of the leaf to the bottom, using a flat shader brush. (Fig. 6)
6. While the base colors are still wet, sideload the dirty brush with Ice Blue. To create individual vein sections, pat blend the color on the leaf. To pat blend, stroke on color in short, overlapping strokes. On the right (light) side of the leaf, pat the Ice Blue from the center vein towards the edge. On the left (dark) side, place the Ice Blue from the outside edge and stroke in towards the center vein. The color will gradually soften as you stroke away from the starting point. (Fig. 7)
7. To sharpen the vein lines, load the chisel edge of the flat brush or a liner brush with Ice Blue. Stroke clean, sharp vein lines down the center and on the sides. Let dry. (Fig. 8)
8. Place accents of True Burgundy + Burnt Umber on the edges of some leaves. To accent, sideload a flat brush with water and accent mix and lightly stroke a color wash on the leaf edges. Wipe color off brush. Blend. (Fig. 8)

Apples:
The apple is painted with a wet-into-wet technique. Work one apple at a time.

1. Mix equal amounts of True Burgundy + Burnt Umber to make a burnt red.
2. Apply Blending Gel Medium to an entire apple.
3. Double load a flat shader with burnt red mix and Napthol Crimson. Stroke brush on the palette to soften color. Place burnt red mix on the outside edge of the apple below the "smile" line. Apply pressure as you stroke this color into the Blending Gel. Also place the burnt red mix at the smile line of the apple. (Fig. 1)
4. Wipe the brush. Load a thin line of Napthol Crimson at the top of the apple. (Fig. 1)
5. Fill in the stem area with Yellow Medium. (Fig. 2)
6. Fill in the very center of the apple with Napthol Crimson. Stroke blend around the perimeter of the apple to soften the dark shading color into the Napthol Crimson. (Fig. 2)
7. Using a smaller flat shader brush, stroke the red from the back of the apple into the center stem area. Wipe brush. Stroke from the center stem area, pulling the Yellow Medium outward. Pick up additional Yellow Medium on the brush as needed to keep the stem area bright. (Fig. 3)
8. To establish the highlight area, pat a ring of Red Light on the upper left side of the apple. Blend. (Fig. 3) Over this highlight, add a smaller ring of Yellow Medium. Blend. (Fig. 4) Add a smaller highlight of Titanium White over the yellow highlight. Blend. Let dry.
9. *Optional:* If you wish a stronger highlight, dry brush a wisp of Medium Yellow and Titanium White. Load very little color on the brush.

Branches & Stems:
Paint one small section of the stem at a time.

1. Apply Blending Gel to one section of the branch.
2. Place Titanium White in the center of the branch. (Fig. 1) Outline both sides with thin lines of Burnt Umber. (Fig. 3)
3. Using a small flat shader, brush stroke an arching curve from the Burnt Umber bottom edge towards the opposite side. (Fig. 3) Wipe brush. Stroke from the top down in the same arching curve. (Fig. 4)
4. Continue this procedure down the entire length of the branch and stems.
5. When all the branches have been blended, overstroke some areas with darker streaks of Burnt Umber, placing more color on the brush and streaking color in a curve. (Fig. 4)

Tendrils:
Mix Yellow Medium + the yellow-green leaf mix. Thin with water to an inky consistency. Paint curlicues and tendrils with a script liner brush.

Apple Worksheet

Apple & Branch:

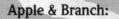

Fig. 1. Apply Blending Gel to entire apple. Double load flat brush with Napthol Crimson and burnt red mix. Stroke on perimeter of apple and on "smile" line.

Fig. 2. Fill in stem area with Medium Yellow and Napthol Crimson on top edge and the very center of the apple. Coat branch with Blending Gel Medium. Fill center with Titanium White. Outline with Burnt Umber.

Fig. 3. Blend colors. Begin to establish highlight by blending a circular shape of Red Light. Pull red into stem center then Yellow out. Stroke the branch from the bottom up in curving stroke.

Fig. 4. Strengthen highlight by blending in Yellow Medium, then Titanium White. Stroke branch from top to bottom.

Leaf:

Fig. 5. Fill in leaf with Blending Gel Medium. Double load flat brush with yellow-green mix and Pure Black. Place dark shading. Fill in with Medium Yellow and yellow-green mix at top edge.

Fig. 6. Blend colors from top of leaf to bottom and bottom to top on each side of center vein.

Fig. 7. Establish side vein sections by pat blending with Ice Blue. Stroke Ice Blue on the right side from the center vein out and on the left side from the outside edge in.

Fig. 8. Add vein lines with Ice Blue. Let dry. Sideload a brush with burnt red mix and wash color on the edges.

$\mathcal{F}$ull $\mathcal{R}$oses & $\mathcal{B}$uds painted by $\mathcal{H}$eather $\mathcal{R}$edick

*The book **Zhostovo** introduced us to an intriguing technique of Russian Painting. This lovely decorative plate features Full Roses. It was published by Plaid Enterprises, Inc. in 1997.*

Heather is best known for her painting techniques of the Zhostovo folk art style. In 1986, during a tour of the Soviet Union as a Canadian Delegate to the Performing Arts, Heather was introduced to Russian art and the Zhostovo style. In 1994, through the efforts of Priscilla Hauser, came the opportunity to meet and paint with Larisa Dyatlova. This was the beginning of a new, exciting change in Heather's painting. Today, Heather Redick teaches the Zhostovo technique throughout Canada and operates a retail/wholesale decorative arts business featuring her books, her brush line, videos, and custom wood surfaces.

Heather's greatest joy comes from teaching as she travels throughout Canada, the United States, Japan, and other countries. Heather encourages membership in both CDAN (Canadian Decorative Artists' Network) and The National Society of Decorative Painters, two organizations offering new ideas, links and education for the decorative artist.

Heather and her husband Robert reside in Zurich, Ontario, Canada, and have two grown children, Kimberly and Craig, and four English Setters (Victoria, Andrew, Alexandra and Henryetta). Use the postcard option on her web site to send greetings to others, especially canine fanciers.

Please feel free to contact Heather in writing anytime at: Heather Redick, The Tole Booth, Box 304, Zurich, ON, Canada, N0M 2T0; or e-mail her at: heather@hay.net You can view her work at her web site: www.HeatherRedick.com.

Heather Redick Painting Techniques

Loading Your Brush

- In order to paint the strokes, your brush must be properly loaded with paint. Working on a wet palette will allow the necessary time for blending. A dry palette won't give you the wet time to blend properly.

- Before loading with paint, wet brush with water. Touch brush on an absorbent towel to remove the loose water. If you leave too much water in your brush, the paint will become too diluted. Don't rub the brush – you will damage the hairs.

- Use your palette knife to keep paint puddles neat and make loading easier.

- Be sure to pick up adequate paint on the brush. (I've found that most people don't load enough paint on their brushes.)

Full Load

Load the brush this way for most strokes.
1. Load filbert brush with water. With the brush flat on the surface of the palette, pull paint into the bristles from the side of your puddle of paint.
2. Move to another part of the palette and work the paint into the bristles. Replenish with paint as you blend until the brush is fully and evenly loaded. Make sure not to change the shape (the chisel) of your brush. If you load too much paint, wipe the flat outside hairs on your towel and re-coat from the blending area of the palette.

Side Load

Load the brush this way when you want to float color.
1. Load filbert brush with water. Flatten the brush on the palette. Pull one side of the brush through the edge of your paint puddle. Be sure to pick up adequate paint.
2. Move to another part of your palette and blend the paint into the brush. be sure not to let the paint move across the whole brush.

Full Roses and Buds

by Heather Redick

1 Gather These Supplies

FolkArt® Artists' Pigments:
Raw Sienna #452
Sap Green #458
Alizarin Crimson #758
Titanium White #480
Yellow Medium #455
Payne's Gray #477

FolkArt® Acrylic Colors:
Licorice #938
Bluebell #909
Raspberry Sherbet #966
Hunter Green #406

FolkArt® Metallic Acrylic Colors:
Pure Gold #660
Inca Gold #676

Project Surface:
Chippendale wooden plate,
    11-1/2"

2 Prepare the Surface

Read General Instructions before beginning.
1. Prepare wood.
2. Basecoat plate with Licorice. Let dry.
3. Trace and transfer pattern.

3 Paint the Design

Important: Refer to the appropriate worksheets for painting leaves and flowers.

Leaves:
1. Undercoat with Titanium White.
2. Base green leaves with Sap Green. Base copper leaves with Raw Sienna.
3. Shadow with Alizarin Crimson and Sap Green + Payne's Gray.
4. Add layered strokes to green leaves with Sap Green + Yellow Medium.
5. Add layered strokes to copper leaves with Raw Sienna + Yellow Medium.

Full Roses:
1. Undercoat with Titanium White.
2. Base pink rose with Raspberry Sherbet. Base white rose with Bluebell.
3. Follow instructions with Full Rose Painting Worksheet.
4. Dot centers with Alizarin Crimson and Yellow Medium.

Pattern – Enlarge 200% for actual size

Buds:
1. Undercoat with Titanium White.
2. Base bud petals with Raspberry Sherbet.
3. Base calyxes with Sap Green.

Filler Strokes:
Brush mix Raw Sienna + Yellow Medium to create a rust tone. Paint filler strokes.

Border:
1. Mix equal amounts Inca Gold + Pure Gold. Paint gold part of border, stroke by stroke.
2. Paint green part of border with Hunter Green.

4 Finish

Apply three coats of varnish. ❑

LEAF WORKSHEET #1

Single Green Leaf:

1. Undercoat

2. Basecoat

3. Shadow vein with 1st shadow color

4. Shadow end with 1st shadow color

5. Add 2nd shadow color

6. Add 1st layer of strokes

7. Add 2nd layer of strokes

8. Add 3rd layer strokes and outlines

Single Orange Leaf:

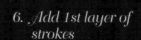

1. Undercoat

2. Basecoat

3. Shadow vein with 1st shadow color

4. Shadow end with 1st shadow color

5. Add 2nd and 3rd shadow color

6. Add 1st layer of strokes

7. Add 2nd layer of strokes

8. Add 3rd layer strokes and outlines

Small Paired Leaves:

1. After under-coating, basecoat each leaf with a different color

2. Shade ends of leaves with 1st shadow color. Shade across centers with 2nd shadow color

3. Add 1st layers of strokes

4. Add 2nd layers of strokes and outlines

Redick '97

Painting a Full Rose

Step 1. Trace and transfer the pattern.

Trace the pattern and carefully transfer the pattern lines. At this point, you need only transfer the outsides of the petal shapes and perhaps the shape of the upper bowl and the outside lower bowl. (See the rose at the upper right on the Rose Worksheet.) Remember the pattern lines are there only to guide your eyes and hands, and need not be adhered to exactly.

Step 2. Undercoat.

Use this opportunity to practice your strokes and feel the shape of the flower and petals. See Fig. 1.
1. Carefully load your filbert brush with Titanium White. (I used a size 10 brush.)
2. Stroke on undercoat, beginning at bottom center. See the Rose Worksheet, where the strokes are numbered in order. I pull these strokes, so I turn the piece so the flower is upside down. Do not turn your brush during these strokes.
3. Paint the side strokes. I turn the piece to paint these strokes, alternating from side to side, carefully creating shape. Press down and allow the brush time to spread. Touch and press gently. Carefully pull and lift, moving your strokes toward the bottom center of the large bowl.
4. Paint the top of the flower with straight, wisped strokes.
5. Fill in the center with two or three flat strokes moving in a slightly rounded motion from side to side. Some roses require more strokes, others fewer to fill in the shape.

Step 3. Basecoat.

Basecoat the flower with the color specified in the individual project instructions, using the same strokes used to paint the undercoat. The basecoat should achieve solid coverage. See Fig. 2. Here, the basecoat is Bluebell.

Step 4. Float shadows.

Float the important shadows in place. On the leaves, two colors or color mixes are used to shade the rose. See Fig. 2.
1. Float several coats Alizarin Crimson across the top, in and around the small bowl, and around both sides of the large bowl. (This takes time.)
2. Add a brush mix of Alizarin Crimson, Sap Green, and Payne's Gray to deepen the shadow and add color. See the example at upper right on the Rose Worksheet, ignoring the dotted lines indicating the two bowls.

Step 5. Add the first layer of strokes.

Note the direction of each stroke on the Rose Worksheet. See Fig. 3.
1. Load brush with color. Choose colors with very little contrast to the basecoat or brush mix some of the basecoat color with a very small amount of Titanium White or any light color. To brush mix, load your brush with the basecoat color, dip in the lighter color, and move to another area of your palette and blend into the brush.
2. Stroke color(s), following the stroke pattern used for undercoating for strokes 1 through 8.
3. Float strokes 9 through 16 into place.

Step 6. Paint cupped petals.

Using the same color or color mix, paint the cupped petals in the center according to the numbered strokes on the Rose Worksheet. If you're not comfortable painting these strokes freehand, position your pattern and lightly transfer the petals' location and shape. See Fig. 4.

Step 7. Add second layer of strokes.

Using a slightly lighter color, add the second layer of strokes. See Full Rose Worksheet, Fig. 5.

Step 8. Add floated side strokes to cupped petals.

Add floated side strokes in the lighter color to the top of each of the cupped petals, moving from the inside of the flower out towards the bottom of the floated side petals, connecting to them. See Full Rose Worksheet, Fig. 5.

Step 9. Add third layer of strokes.

1. Add a third layer of strokes in a slightly lighter color, remembering to make your wisping strokes shorter. In the third layer, you're only highlighting the lighter petals. (The top, side, and back petals should be darker, and were probably complete with one or two layers of strokes.)
2. Reinforce the light color on the cupped petals, again with shorter wisps, highlighting the beginning of the stroke. Continue layering overstrokes on the petals until you have achieved the desired contrast/highlight. See Fig. 6.

Step 10. Re-float the shadow colors.

Re-float the shadow colors back in to separate the petals and petal groups from each other and to separate the outside and back petals from the cupped center petals. You don't need to match the colors of the first shadows – you can add more or less of a color of your own choice. See Fig. 7.

Step 11. Add defining strokes.

1. Load your script liner with the light color and/or any other petal colors.
2. Stroke from the center out to the bottom edge of the outside petals. See Fig. 8.
3. *Optional step:* Add extra strokes in between the petals, following the shape of the flower.

Step 12. Outline the petals.

See Step 7 in "Painting Leaves" section and Full Rose Worksheet, Fig. 8.

Step 13. Paint flower centers.

Painting flower centers is fun. You can choose just about any center, from a simple dot to a more detailed one, and use it in any flower. Study all the Painting Worksheets for examples.

Step 14. Glaze *(Optional)*.

Use glazing if you need to darken strokes or the back of the flower.
1. Dampen the entire flower.
2. Glaze the area you wish to change with a very thin wash of paint color.

Step 15. Clean up.

Clean up around your flowers, if necessary, with the background color.

Rose Worksheet

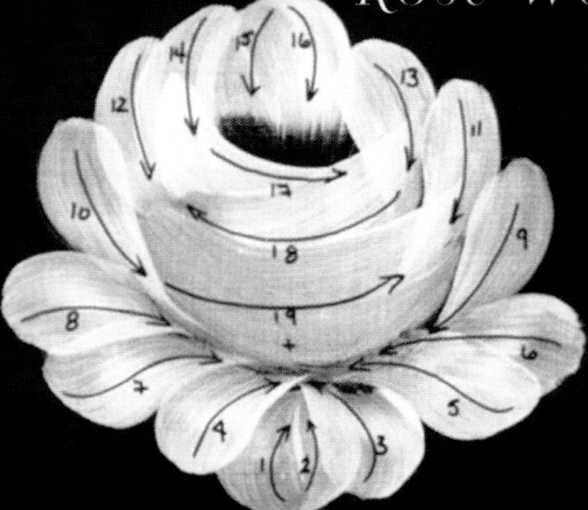

Fig. 1.
Undercoat.

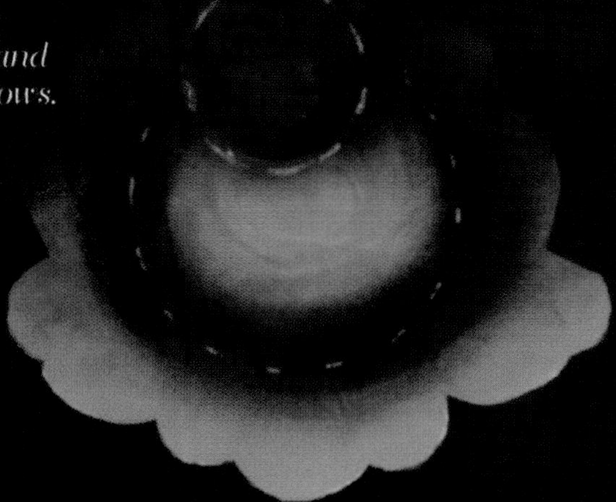

Fig. 2.
Basecoat and float shadows.

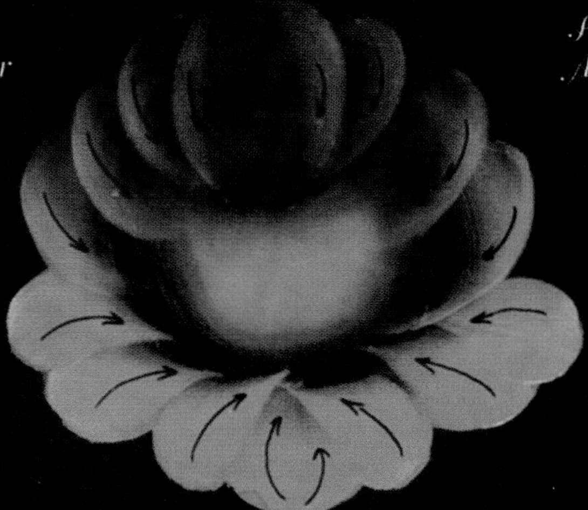

Fig. 3.
Add 1st layer strokes.

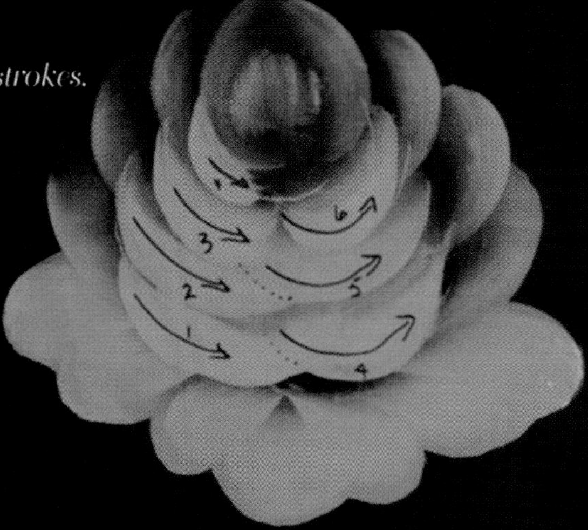

Fig. 4.
Add cupped strokes.

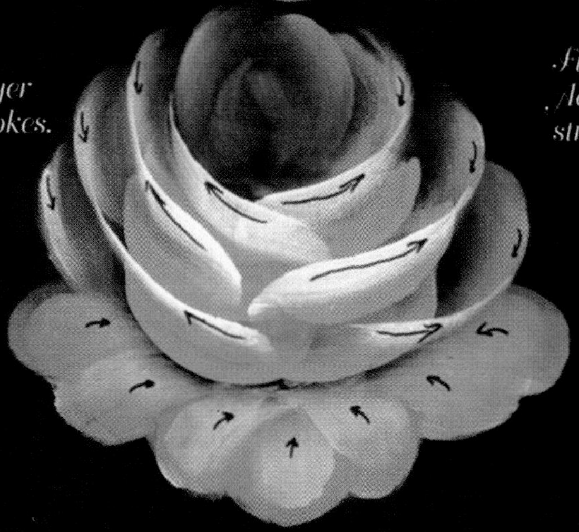

Fig. 5.
Add 2nd layer and side strokes.

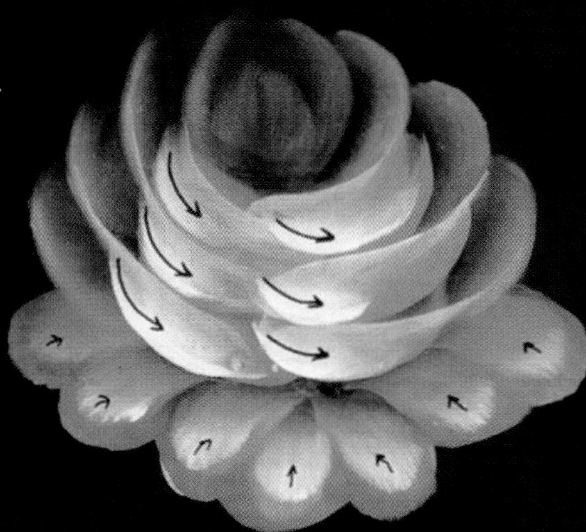

Fig. 6.
Add third layer strokes.

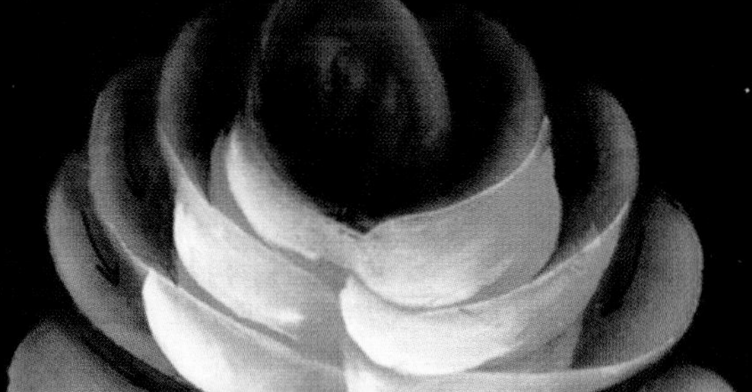

Fig. 7.
Re-float shadows.

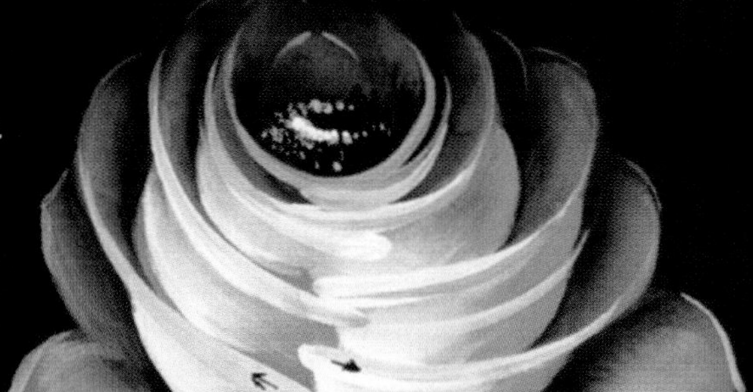

Fig. 8.
Add defining strokes. Outline. Paint center.

Redick '97

*S*pringtime *W*ildflowers

painted by *F*aith *R*ollins

This charming birdhouse appeared in Faith's 29th book with Plaid Enterprises, Inc. **Birdhouses and More** *was published in 1997 and has delighted many artists with it's easy and beautiful painting projects.*

*F*aith Rollins began painting in the 1980's with two friends — using this as a social time. Little did she know that this would lead to a full-time career. Over the years Faith's style evolved and became stylized. This style is recognizable as Faith's country folk art style. During her career, Faith has authored over 30 books for Plaid; designed a line of wood products; designed a line of stencils. Early in her career she and her husband, Larry, designed and sold unfinished wood pieces and other products to painters. Faith is currently designing product for the gift market. She also taught seminars throughout the United States and Taiwan.

Faith and her husband Larry live in Shawnee, Kansas. They have two married children and a brood of spoiled grandchildren.

Faith's 6-Step Procedure

Step 1 – Paint the Design

Transfer painting pattern to the wood item. Paint the project using the colors and techniques given in the individual project instructions.

Step 2 – Sand After Painting

On some projects, you will sand the piece all over, sanding heavier in some areas to remove more of the paint to get a weathered look. Some of the projects in this book are just lightly sanded and are not as primitive as others. Wipe with a tack cloth after sanding.

Step 3 – Flyspeck Your Project

Flecking or flyspecking is done after sanding. You can use a stencil brush, palette knife, and Licorice paint (unless project directions specify another color) or a Decorator Products™ Spatter Tool (#30121 by Plaid®) with Licorice paint. You may want to practice before working with your project (see worksheet). In order to flyspeck, follow these steps:

1. Work the paint into the stencil brush or into the stiff bristle brush that comes with the spatter tool, being careful not to have your paint too thin.
2. Point brush at project. If using a stencil brush, draw palette knife across the bristles, pulling it up toward you, moving the brush around the project as needed to get the specks where you want them. When using the Spatter Tool, pull the brush along the screen wire, moving slowly. If specks are too tiny, the brush was not loaded with enough paint. If specks are soaking into the wood, the paint has too much water.
3. Allow flyspecking to dry.

Step 4 – Apply Antiquing

Before antiquing, lightly mist your painted project two or three times with Matte Acrylic Sealer.

Using either a prepared antiquing medium or one of your own favorite formulas and a sponge brush, cover the entire piece with antiquing.

Step 5 – Wipe Off Antiquing

Remove the antiquing immediately by gently wiping with a soft rag or paper towels. At this point it is up to you as to how dark you want your project. It should be rubbed lighter in the center, working out to the edges. If edges are too light, you can go back with your rag dipped into full strength antiquing and wipe it on front from the outside edge toward the middle. Be sure to blend carefully.

Step 6 – Spray Again for Protection

Allow the wood piece to dry 24 to 48 hours, then lightly mist again two or three times with Matte Acrylic Sealer. Remember to always finish the backside of your project.

Tips and Techniques

Basecoat

When basecoating, apply a solid coat of paint to the entire piece. Do not try to go around the design areas and then paint the design along the edges of the basecoat as this will cause ridges. This is why I generally basecoat all Santas with Tapioca, for instance. When you transfer the pattern, the undercoat for all hair and fur is already there.

Wash

This simply means to add a lot of water to your paint and apply it over your basecoat in order to add a transparent color for the sky or ground, for example.

Sideload

Use as large a brush as you are comfortable with when sideloading. I prefer to use angular brushes, but flats work very well.

Dip your brush into water and blot on a paper towel, leaving some water in your brush. Dip the long corner of an angular brush (or the corner of a flat brush) into paint and blend on your palette. If loaded and blended correctly, you will have a gradual change from paint on one side to clear water on the opposite side.

Floats

Floating is used for shading and highlighting. Remember to use a wide brush.

First dampen with water the area you are going to float. Sideload your brush with the appropriate color and apply the paint to the dampened area. When floating, do not overwork an area. Allow to dry completely before refloating. You may need to apply two or three floats before the shading is dark enough or the highlights are bright enough. Make the first float the widest and each successive float more narrow than the previous.

Stipple

Use either a deerfoot brush, a very old "fuzzy" brush, or a very soft stencil brush for stippling. The size of the brush will depend on the size of the area on which you are working.

Dip a dry brush into paint. Wipe out almost all of the paint on a paper towel (a circular motion works very well). Pounce or tap the paint onto the project. Usually, there will be several stages of stippling, as for fur, where you will change colors each time. Be sure to keep stippling in a light and airy manner to allow some of each color to show through.

Flyspecking

Flyspecking is used to obtain an old look, to darken some areas, or just to add character to the project. I prefer to use a Decorator Tools™ Spatter Tool to flyspeck.

Dip the stiff bristle brush into water and blot out almost all of the water on a paper towel. Dip the brush into paint, working the paint into the bristles by tapping on your palette. Point the wire screen toward the area you want to flyspeck and pull the brush across the screen to flip the top of the bristles and send "splatters" of paint onto your project. Cover with a paper towel any areas you do not want to flyspeck. You may want to spray your project with Matte Acrylic Sealer before flyspecking. This will enable you to wipe off any splatters that are unappealing. If you spray before fly-specking, you will still need to spray again before antiquing.

If you cannot find the Spatter Tool, you can use a stencil brush or a toothbrush for this technique. Simply dip brush in paint and point it towards projects. Use a palette knife to rake across the brush, splattering your project with specks of paint.

Dots

Make dots with the handle end of a paint brush or with a stylus. To make descending size dots, dip the handle into paint and dot three or four times before reloading. To make all dots the same size, dip the brush handle into paint each time you make a dot. To make folk art hearts, place two dots of the same size side by side, barely touching. Using the small tip of a stylus or a 10/0 script liner, pull down the point of the heart.

Linework

When adding linework, use a script liner in a size that is appropriate to the area you are painting. I usually use a 10/0 script liner for outlining and maybe a little larger size for scrollwork.

Thin the paint with a little water until it is the consistency of ink. Load your brush and roll it on your palette, bringing the brush tip to a fine point. Use only the tip of the brush when making fine lines.

Worn-Look Sanding

This simply means to sand the paint away down to the raw wood. This is done mostly on the edges, heavier in some places than others. The result is an "old" look which becomes highly visible when you antique. It is sometimes called "rough sanding" in this book.

Antiquing

I usually prefer to use FolkArt® Waterbase Antiquing on my projects unless the piece is stained.

After spraying the piece with Matte Acrylic Sealer, brush the antiquing over the project. Wipe off the excess with a soft paper towel. Wiping from the center out with a circular motion, continue to wipe off the antiquing; leave it darker toward the outer edges. If the piece is still too dark, dampen a paper towel and wipe again. Be sure to clean up the brighter areas with a damp paper towel. You may wish to go back and repaint your highlights to help them pop out after you have antiqued. ❏

Springtime Wildflowers

By Faith Rollins

1 Gather These Supplies:

FolkArt® Acrylic Colors:
Licorice #938
Slate Blue #910
Teal Green #733
Tapioca #903
Country Twill #602
Real Brown #231
Honeycomb #942
Indigo #908
Huckleberry #745
Wrought Iron #925
English Mustard #959
Sunflower #432
Nutmeg #944

Other Supplies Needed:
Wood tissue cabinet, 7" x 5-1/2" x 24"
Top, bottom, and sides cut from 3/4"
   pine according to pattern
Door cut from 3/8" Baltic birch
   according to pattern
Wooden door knob, 3/4"
Pine scrap (for closure tab),
   1/4" x 1/2" x 1"
2 metal hinges, 1"
FolkArt® Matte Acrylic Sealer #788 (6
   oz.) or #789 (12 oz.)
Decorator Tools™ Spatter Tool #30121
Sand paper & tack cloth
Shiva Burnt Umber oil paint and
   Norwegian Painting Medium
Wood glue
Small nails

2 Prepare Surface

1. Assemble cabinet.
2. Basecoat cabinet, knob, and closure
   tab with Slate Blue + Teal Green.
3. Sand cabinet, sanding heavier around
   the edges. Also sand knob and closure
   tab. Wipe all with a tack cloth.
4. Basecoat the door of cabinet with 2
   coats of Tapioca, sanding between
   coats.
5. Transfer the pattern to the door.

3 Paint The Design

Fence
1. Paint the fence Country Twill; shade
   with a float of Chocolate Fudge.

Birdhouse
1. Paint the pole Honeycomb; shade with

Real Brown.
2. Paint the birdhouse Slate Blue + Teal
   Green; shade with Indigo.
3. Paint the roof and base of birdhouse
   Huckleberry; highlight with Huckleberry + Tapioca.
4. Paint the entrance holes and perches
   Licorice.
5. Shade under the perches with a float
   of Indigo.
6. Highlight the perches with Licorice +
   Tapioca.
7. Shade inside the entrance holes with
   thinned Slate Blue + Teal Green +
   Licorice.
8. Paint the board lines on the side house
   and indicate a crackled effect on the
   center birdhouse with thinned
   Indigo.

Greenery and Flowers
1. Paint the grass, weeds, and vine with
   Wrought Iron.
2. Dab Wrought Iron on some of the
   weeds to indicate leaves.
3. Paint the leaves on the vine Wrought
   Iron.
4. Paint the flowers with a double load
   of English Mustard and Sunflower.
5. Dab the flower centers Huckleberry.
6. Add a highlight to the flower centers
   with Huckleberry + Tapioca.
7. Shade next to the centers on the petals
   with a float of Nutmeg.

Birds
1. Paint the three flying birds Licorice.

4 Finish

1. Flyspeck cabinet door with Licorice.
2. Lightly spray with Matte Acrylic Sealer.
3. Antique with Shiva Burnt Umber oil
   paint and Norwegian Painting
   Medium, wiping out the highlights
   and darkening along the edges.
4. Thin the Burnt Umber paint with the
   painting medium and stain the inside
   of the cabinet.
5. Attach door to cabinet with hinges.
6. Attach knob to door and closure tab to
   cabinet, referring to photo for placement.
7. Rub Burnt Umber oil paint on all
   metal pieces to antique. ❏

**Pattern Enlarge 200%
for actual size**

Dogwood in Spring

painted by Gigi Smith Burns

*This decorative glass project painted with acrylics was enjoyed by many. This dogwood vase is from the book **Painting on Glass** published by Plaid.*

Gigi Smith-Burns has a great love of teaching and has been teaching decorative art for over 26 years. When her students successfully complete beautiful pieces it brings smiles and warm fuzzy feelings to her heart. She believes that everyone can learn to paint beautiful pieces with good teachers and a desire to learn.

Gigi has recently authored her fifteenth book, entitled, THE GARDEN PATH. She has designed over 200 pattern packets, co-authored 14 books, and written numerous magazine articles. Gigi teaches at conventions and chapters all around the country.

You may contact this artist at:

Gigi Smith-Burns
2274 King James Ct.
Winter Park, FL 32792
or call 407-671-6220
or e-mail her at GigiSmBurn@aol.com

Gigi's Painting Techniques

These are two techniques I use frequently.

Shimmer Technique: Use a sideloaded flat brush that has been softened on the palette. Place the brush down and float color where you wish the shimmer to be. Quickly reverse the process by flipping the brush over and floating color against the color that was just placed. This will make a shimmer effect, with the outside fading out and the center of the shimmer the brightest.

Pivot Cheek Technique: Use a flat brush or angle brush. Dip in water or Extender. Load one side of the brush with color specified; do not allow paint to travel across more than one-quarter of the brush. Blend brush on wet palette. With the color side of brush toward the center, gently and quickly walk the color in a circle or half-circle, depending on instructions. Keep the water/extender side of brush toward the outer edge.

TIPS
- I use a 1/2" angle brush for most shading and highlighting.
- For shading and highlighting, I have Extender in my brush, but not a lot. Blot your brush after dipping in Extender.

Dogwood In Spring

By Gigi Smith Burns

1 Gather These Supplies

FolkArt® Acrylic Colors:
Wrought Iron #925
Lemonade #904
Raspberry Sherbet #966
Acorn Brown #941
English Mustard #959
Thicket #924
Real Brown #231
Whipped Berry #759
Maple Syrup #945
Thicket #924
Bayberry #922
Buttercup #905
Rose Chiffon #753
Indigo #908

FolkArt® Artists' Pigments:
Warm White #649

Painting Surface:
4 sided glass jar 9" tall x 6" wide at top

Other Supplies:
FolkArt® Glass & Tile Medium
Raffia

2 Preparation

1. Clean the glass on the jars surface thoroughly. Paint the surface with Folk Art ® Glass & Tile Medium. This will give the surface some "tooth" that allows your paint to adhere to it. You may need a couple of coats.
2. Transfer pattern to glass by tracing the pattern onto tracing paper, and positioning it on the glass. Slip a piece of graphite paper between the traced pattern and the glass surface. Holding securely, trace the pattern to transfer the pattern to glass.

3 Paint the Design

Dogwood Blossoms:
Base paint with Warm White. Shade with a mix of Real Brown + a touch of Raspberry Wine. Base centers with Buttercup. Shade Centers with English Mustard. Dot seeds with Wrought Iron.

Branches:
Base with Acorn Brown. Randomly Shade with Maple Syrup. Also randomly shade with Wrought Iron.

Leaves:
Base with Bayberry. Shade with Thicket. Highlight with Lemonade. Tint with Rose Chiffon. Deepen Shading with Wrought Iron.

Bird Nest:
Base with Acorn Brown. Streak in the following colors: Buttercup, Maple Syrup, Wrought Iron. Shade inside the nest with Wrought Iron. Paint eggs with sideloaded Whipped Berry.

Bird:
Base with Whipped Berry. Shade with Indigo. Highlight with Whipped Berry + a touch of Warm White. Base beak with Buttercup and shade with English Mustard. Paint Licorice dot eye and add a small highlight dot to it with Warm White.

Squiggles:
Paint with Bayberry.

Backshading:
Shade behind nest and bird with Wrought Iron. Let painting dry.

4 Finish

1. Coat painted area with FolkArt® Glass & Tile Medium.
2. Tie several strands of raffia around neck of jar, tying ends in a knot. ❑

Pattern is actual size

Floral Welcome Pattern

Instructions on page 112

**Enlarge 200%
for actual size**

Floral Welcome

painted by Chris Stokes

*One of many popular books, **In the Garden** appeared in 1996 published by Plaid Enterprises, Inc. In this book as in all of Chris' work, she offers enchanting and imaginative projects to paint.*

Chris Stokes has been painting for almost two decades. She says, "I am a self-taught artist without any fancy credentials, but I do love to paint." And as you see, her work speaks for itself.

In 1984 Chris opened a quaint little craft/gift/antique shop nestled in downtown Dallas, GA called *The Craft Cottage*. With much hard work and self education, this shop is now a thriving business of gifts, antiques, and of course, a selection of various hand painted items.

Chris says that "Living in a log home in Dallas Georgia with my husband Ron makes life lots of fun." Chris speaks proudly of two new additions to the family, besides her son James and his wife Mitzi and her daughter Jennifer and Jennifer's husband Bruce. The two new additions are Linzi and Deven, two beautiful granddaughters that are "...just too precious!" "We may be looking at two budding artists/ authors a few years down the road," she says. "And my cats, dogs, and horses complete my family."

For information on classes and supplies, contact:
The Craft Cottage
222 Main Street
Dallas, GA 30132
Phone: 770-445-8228
We would love to hear from you. Please call or send a self-addressed stamped envelope for inquiries.

Painting Stroke Roses

Floral Welcome Sign

∞

by Chris Stokes

1 Gather These Supplies

FolkArt® Acrylic Colors:
Taffy #902
Hunter Green #406
Pure Gold (metallic)#660
Christmas Red #958
Autumn Leaves #920
Buttercream #614
School Bus Yellow #736
Licorice #938
Old Ivy #927
Rose Garden #754
Wicker White #901

FolkArt® Artists' Pigments:
Prussian Blue #486
Dioxazine Purple #463
Burnt Sienna #943
Burnt Carmine #686
Burnt Umber #462

Painting Surface:
Wooden Sign, cut from 1/2" pine
following pattern

Brushes:
Angular Brush 3/8"
Liner Brush #2
Flat Shader Brushes #8, #10
Round Brush #3
Sponge Brush 2"
Toothbrush
Stylus
Natural Sea Sponge

Other Supplies:
FolkArt® Antiquing Medium: Down
Home Brown
FolkArt® Waterbase Varnish
21" of mauve braided roping
Fine Sand Paper
Tack Cloth

2 Preparation

1. Sand and wipe off the wooden plaque with a tack cloth.
2. Stain wood with a sponge brush and inky Down Home Brown antiquing. Let dry.
3. Using Taffy and a touch of Christmas Red + Autumn Leaves, sponge the front surface with a sea sponge. Let dry.
4. "Sand" with brown paper
5. Spatter with inky Old Ivy
6. Transfer the pattern

3 Paint the Design

Transparent Leaves:
Using a brush with plenty of water, side-load some Old Ivy, the Burnt Carmine, then Prussian Blue. Keep these colors very transparent. Paint some leaves with just one of these colors and others with two or all three colors.

Blue Flowers (on left):
Double Load a #10 flat brush with Prussian Blue/Taffy. Wiggle in flowers. Pounce Burnt Umber in the center; then using a stylus, dot with School Bus Yellow.

Peach Flowers:
Double load a #10 flat brush with Christmas Red + Autumn Leaves/Taffy to paint each petal. Outline petals with Wicker White. Pounce in the centers with Burnt Umber and Old Ivy. Paint stamen lines with Burnt Umber. Make dots with stylus, using School Bus Yellow and Taffy.

Burgundy Rose:
Double Load a #10 flat brush with Burnt Carmine/Buttercream. Paint rose as shown for Stroke Roses on page 111.

Peach Rose:
Double load brush with Christmas Red + Autumn Leaves/Taffy + a touch of Wicker White. Paint rose and bud in the same manner.

Sunflower:
Pounce in center with Burnt Umber and Burnt Sienna. Highlight by pouncing in a touch of School Bus Yellow. Double load a #8 flat brush with Burnt Sienna/School Bus Yellow and paint bottom of petals. Paint top petals with School Bus Yellow/Taffy.

Daisy:
Pounce in center with School Bus Yellow and Burnt Sienna. Shade with floated Burnt Umber. Pull in bottom petals with a #5 round brush and inky Taffy. Pull in top petals with Wicker White. Make dots around center with a stylus using Burnt Umber, School Bus Yellow, and Wicker White.

Pansies:
Paint with a double loaded #10 flat brush. For purple pansy, use Dioxazine Purple/Wicker White. For mauve pansy, use Rose Garden/Taffy. Paint throats with inky Licorice. Add comma strokes and dots with School Bus Yellow.

Leaves:
Use both #8 and #10 double loaded flat shaders. Refer to the photo of the project and paint with Old Ivy/School Bus Yellow. Add a touch of Taffy for some and a touch of Prussian Blue (on a dirty brush) for others. Also now and then pick up some Burnt Carmine, Hunter Green, and a touch of Buttercream.

Filler Flowers:
Double load an angular brush with Prussian Blue/Wicker White for some and Rose Garden/Wicker White for others.

Squiggles and Comma Strokes:
Inky Pure Gold on a liner brush

Lettering:
Paint comma stroke type lettering with a #2 liner brush and Licorice. Let dry. Shadow letters on right side with sideloaded Pure Gold.

4 Finish

1. Varnish with water base varnish
2. Staple ends of mauve braid to back side of sign for hanging. An alternative, if desired, is to attach a stake to back of sign and place it in your flower garden. ❑

❧ General Stroke Pansy ❧

Double load brush with colors indicated in project instructions.
"Wiggle" in each petal, reloading after each.
Double load to form tiny "lip" on folded over petals.

❧ Throat ❧

Pull Licorice (or colors indicated) with a liner or rake brush.
Add comma stroke and tiny throat lines with yellow color indicated.

❧ Leaves ❧

Double load brush with colors indicated in
project instructions. "Wiggle" in leaves,
forming veins.

St. Nick's Sweet Stash

painted by Prudy Vannier

*This little fellow came about in the book **12 Joys of Christmas** published in 1995 by Plaid Enterprises, Inc.*

Prudy Vannier resides in Northville Michigan, with her husband, Jim, and their four children. She designs decorative painting projects and teaches her techniques to painters in her home studio at Which Craft in Livonia Michigan, and around the country by invitation.

Prudy has a degree in art education but learned decorative painting skills from the many classes and conventions sponsored by the National Society of Decorative Painters.

To Contact this Artist:
Prudy Vannier
270 Maplewood
Northville, Michigan 48167

Knit Ribbing

1. Float to shade across top of ribbing.

2. Line ribbing. Float to deepen shading.

3. Fill in segments here and there with highlight color.

Candy

1. Basecoat

2. Add color

3. Shade

4. Highlight candy canes on the right. Float Wicker White to make wrappers.

Bear

1. Basecoat. Pounce Raw Sienna to shade.

2. Deepen shading with Burnt Umber. Highlight by pouncing Taffy.

3. Tint by lightly pouncing other colors on your palette. Add facial features with a liner.

St. Nick's Box

By Prudy Vannier

1 Gather These Supplies

FolkArt® Acrylic Colors:

Light Flesh #229	Terracotta #433
Taffy #902	Dapple Gray #937
Old Ivy #927	Teddy Bear Tan #419
Primrose #930	Wicker White #901
Teal #405	Licorice #938
Barnwood #936	Glazed Carrots #741
Calico Red #932	Green #408
Cardinal Red #414	

FolkArt® Artists' Pigments:

Raw Sienna #452	Burnt Carmine #686
Burnt Umber #462	Portrait #422

Painting Surface:
Wood Santa Box, 8" x 13-1/2" x 2-1/4" deep

Other Supplies:
Medium wood Stain
FolkArt® Water Base Antiquing: Wood'n Bucket Brown
Snow Texture Medium
Folk Art® Satin Water Base Varnish
Hot glue gun and glue sticks
Fine sandpaper

2 Preparation

1. Sand the box and wipe clean
2. Stain the inside compartment, inside of lid, and the bottom. Let dry.
3. Seal wood with a light coat of varnish. Let dry.
4. Transfer pattern lightly onto the lid. Extend the basic lines of pattern over the sides of the box as indicated on pattern.

3 Paint the Design

Basecoating:
1. Hat, suit, sides, and top of inside-Cardinal Red
2. Face-Light Flesh
3. Hair and beard - Barnwood
4. Bear-Teddy Bear Brown
5. Cinnamon sticks-Calico Red
6. Remainder of candy (do not basecoat the wrappers) and the wood knob-Wicker White

Face:
1. Shade under hat, around eyes and under eyebrows with floated Portrait; use a 1/2" angular brush or a #16 flat. Lightly float same color around the nose as well.
2. Float primrose across top of moustache to redden cheeks. Walk it up to cover about two-thirds of the cheeks. Also float Primrose across top of nose.
3. Deepen cheek color across top of moustache by floating Cardinal Red.
4. Fill in eyes with Wicker White. Paint irises with Teal. Paint pupils with Licorice. With a liner brush, paint Wicker White highlights in eyes-a dot on pupils at the 2 o'clock position and a small stroke on irises at the 7 o'clock position.
5. Outline eyes with Terracotta, using a liner brush.
6. Float Wicker White across tops of cheeks and nose. Add Wicker White strokes at corners of cheeks and nose to intensify highlights.
7. Fill in eyebrows with Barnwood. Paint Barnwood eyelashes. Line eyebrows with thinned Wicker White.

Hat:
1. Float across top of knit ribbing with Raspberry Wine. Deepen shading next to ribbing with a more narrow float of Burnt Carmine.
2. Float across top of hat with Glazed Carrots to highlight it. Intensify highlight by floating at very top edge with Cardinal Red + Wicker White.
3. Paint lines in ribbon with Raspberry Wine, using liner brush. Sideload with Glazed Carrots and paint over some of the segments formed with the lines. Sideload with the pink mix and do the same.
4. Float across the top of ribbing with Glazed Carrots.

Suit:
1. Shade suit next to beard and around sleeves with floats of Raspberry Wine. Deepen shading in areas that would have the darkest shadows with floats of Burnt Carmine.
2. Highlight suit with Glazed Carrots, then with Cardinal Red + Wicker White, by sideloading a brush with very little paint and pouncing it into the highlight areas-tops of sleeves and where sleeves are creased at bends of arms.

Beard and Moustache:
1. Thin Wicker White and line the beard and moustache.
2. Float Dapple Gray under moustache and around bear and candy. Tint the float around candy by lightly floating thinned Cardinal Red over it.
3. Paint lower lip with Cardinal Red. Fill in mouth with Burnt Carmine.

Candy:
1. Float Glazed Carrots down right sides of cinnamon sticks.
2. Paint the stripes on cinnamon sticks with Wicker White, using a liner brush.
3. Float Burnt Carmine down left side to shade.
4. Stripe the candy cane and mints with Calico Red. Paint the red stripe around the other candies with Calico Red. Paint the tops of the Christmas Trees in those candies with Green and the trunks with Terracotta.
5. Shade the candies with floats of Old Ivy. This goes on left side of candy cane; it goes across the bottoms of others where they are tucked behind each other and the bear.
6. Highlight candy cane and cinnamon sticks by painting a Wicker White line down right sides just inside edges.
7. Sideload with Wicker White and float the wrappers on the candy. Shade next to the candy on the inside of box with floated Raspberry Wine.

Bear:
1. Using a deerfoot or old scruffy brush, pounce Teddy Bear Tan over the basecoat. Without rinsing brush, dip into Raw Sienna and pounce it in the shade areas-across bottom of face, around muzzle, in ears, under arms, on chest, on legs where they are tucked under mitten, and on the bottom of the visible foot. Don't pounce too much lest everything will blend to the same color. Hit a "happy medium."
2. Deepen shading by pouncing Burnt Umber into the Raw Sienna.
3. Highlight by pouncing Taffy into the Teddy Bear Tan across tops of ears, head, arms, and toes.
4. Tint the bear very lightly by pouncing Burnt Carmine and Old Ivy into the shade areas, Primrose in the cheek area, and Glazed Carrots in the middle value areas. This should be very subtle go lightly.
5. Paint nose and mouth with Burnt Carmine.
6. Paint eyes with Licorice. Highlight with dots of Wicker White.

Mittens:
1. Pounce Green lightly on lower half of top mitten. Use same method as for highlighting the sleeves. This will add a little texture to the mitten so that it looks knit.
2. Paint the ribbed cuffs like the ribbon on the hat-line with Licorice, then add Green into the segments. Float across top of ribbing with Green.

Hat Pompon:
1. Antique the corners by floating Folk Art antiquing. Let dry thoroughly.
2. Varnish with satin water base varnish.
❑

St. Nick's Sweet Stash Pattern

Enlarge 165% for actual size

Diagram of Inside

Santa and Friends

∞

By Pat Wakefield

Instructions on page 122

Pattern
Enlarge 155%
for actual size

*S*anta & *F*riends

painted by *P*at *W*akefield

*This album was in Pat's eighth book of Teddy Bear designs, titled **All About Teddy Bears**. It was published in 1998 by Plaid Enterprises, Inc.*

*P*at Wakefield lives with her husband in the Kansas City area. Decorative Painting got its start in Kansas at Cambridge House, the first Decorative Painting shop in the country. Pat taught classes there, and she has traveled all over this country and Canada teaching seminars and attending conventions. She is the author of 23 books and 39 painting packets for the decorative painter. She is versatile in her painting styles and techniques, painting with tube oils, acrylics, pastels, and watercolors. Her background is in a study of fine arts at The University Of Kansas. Her paintings and articles have been included in several international publications. She is a longtime member of The Society of Decorative Painters, has been a judge in the Society's Certification Program, and taught at several conventions. Pat received her Master Decorative Artist Certification in 1975.

You can contact this artist at:

Pat Wakefield, M.D.A.
P.O. Box 3245
Shawnee Mission, KS 66203
or call 913-649-8318. Pat's e-mail address is pat@patwakefield.com, and her Web site is http://www.patwakefield.com.

Other books by Pat Wakefield

Santa & Friends

MEMORY ALBUM

121

Santa & Friends

∞

by Pat Wakefield

1 Gather These Supplies

FolkArt® Acrylic Colors:
Tapioca #903
Dapple Gray #937
Teddy Bear Tan #419
Teddy Bear Brown #417
Country Twill #602
Engine Red #436
Hunter Green #406
Licorice #938
Thunder Blue #609

FolkArt® Artists' Pigments:
Portrait #422
Yellow Ochre #917
Alizarin Crimson #758
Red Light #629
Burnt Umber #462
Medium Yellow #455

Painting Surface:
Wooden memory album cover,
13" x 13-1/2"

Other Supplies:
FolkArt® Blending Gel Medium #867
FolkArt® ClearCote™ Matte Acrylic
Sealer #789
Special brushes: comb brush, deerfoot
brush

2 Preparation

1. Paint the wood piece, both front and back, with Dapple Gray until well covered. Let dry.
2. Transfer pattern to the surface. (Do not transfer the Santa Claus features.)

3 Paint the Design

Background
1. Darken background with a mix of Hunter Green + Licorice. Lay paint on in a slip-slap fashion, working in one small area at a time. Wipe off some of the paint in the upper area. Blend to a soft splotchy effect.
2. Paint pine branches with several different values of Hunter Green + Licorice. Also use Dapple Gray + Tapioca.

Santa Face:
1. Basecoat face with several coats of Portrait until well covered. Let dry after each coat.
2. Transfer the pattern of facial features to the face.
3. Coat each section of the face with Blending Gel before adding the shading and highlighting. Let each coat dry thoroughly before continuing with other coats. Each section may need several coats of paint. Prepare the paint mixtures for the face:
   Dark Flesh: Portrait + Alizarin Crimson + Burnt Umber
   Light Flesh: Portrait + Tapioca
   Pink cheeks: Portrait + Red Light + Alizarin Crimson
4. Paint the dark areas of the face with the dark flesh mix. Paint the cheeks with the pink mix. Add pink also on the nose. Paint the light areas with the light flesh mix.

Santa Eyes:
1. Paint irises with Thunder Blue + Licorice + Tapioca. Paint pupils and outline the irises with Licorice.
2. Paint the whites of eyes with Tapioca. Darken under lids with the dark flesh mix. Paint the highlights with Tapioca.
3. Paint the eyelash lines with Licorice + Dapple Gray.

Santa Mouth:
1. Paint the opening of the mouth with Burnt Umber.
2. Paint lips with the dark flesh mix + Portrait.

Santa Beard, Hair & Eyebrows:
1. Paint the darkest value first with Dapple Gray. Start with a flat brush and layer on colors, gradually becoming lighter by adding more and more Tapioca to the Dapple Gray. Before you are finished, add the colors with a comb brush.
2. Finish with a fine liner brush and Tapioca paint.

Santa's Coat and Hat:
1. Basecoat the dark red fabric areas with Alizarin + Licorice. Basecoat the light red fabric areas with Red Light. Blend the colors slightly. Several coats will be needed.
2. Basecoat the fur on the hat with Tapioca. Use a comb brush to swirl on the paint. Darken with Tapioca + Dapple Gray. Darken the darkest values further with Dapple Gray + Licorice. Highlight with Tapioca.

Instructions are given for bears in a counter-clockwise order, starting with the gray bear on the upper left.

Gray Bear:
Refer to Bear Painting Worksheet and to Plush Fur on Fur Painting Worksheet. Paint fur with a deerfoot brush.
1. Basecoat with Dapple Gray + Tapioca. Continue to layer on the colors. Gradually lighten as you do by adding more and more Tapioca to the mix.
2. Paint eyes and nose with Licorice. Highlight with Tapioca.

Yellow Bear:
Refer to Puffy Fur on Fur Painting Worksheet.
1. Layer paint colors in the order listed below:
   Basecoat with Country Twill.
   Paint dark areas with Burnt Umber + Teddy Bear Brown.
   Paint the medium value areas with Teddy Bear Brown + Yellow Ochre and with Dapple Gray + Tapioca.
   Paint the light areas with Tapioca + Medium Yellow #455, Tapioca + Yellow Ochre, and Tapioca alone.
2. Facial Features: Paint the outer area of the eyes with Yellow Ochre + Red Light. Paint the inner area of eyes, outlining, nose, and mouth with Licorice. Highlight eyes with Tapioca.
3. Bow: Basecoat dark areas with Alizarin Crimson + Licorice. Basecoat light areas with Red Light. Blend only slightly. Several coats will be needed.

White Bear:

Refer to Bear Painting Worksheet and to Plush Fur on Fur Painting Worksheet. Paint fur with a deerfoot brush.

1. Basecoat with Tapioca + Dapple Gray. Layer on several coats. Gradually lighten the fur by adding more and more Tapioca to the mix.
2. Eyes, nose, and mouth: Paint with Licorice. Highlight with Tapioca.
3. Bow: Paint with Red Light + Tapioca. Highlight with Tapioca.

Brown Bear:

Refer to Worn Fur on Fur Painting Worksheet. Paint fur with a flat brush, round brush, and comb brush.

1. Basecoat with Burnt Umber + Teddy Bear Tan. Darken with Burnt Umber + Licorice. Lighten with Teddy Bear Tan + Tapioca.
2. Eyes and Nose: Licorice.
3. Shirt: Paint green stripes with Hunter Green. Darken them with Hunter Green + Licorice. Paint white stripes with Tapioca. Darken them with Tapioca + Dapple Gray.

Brown and Tan Bear:

Refer to Painting Bear Worksheet and to Plush Fur on Fur Painting Worksheet and paint fur with a deerfoot brush.

1. Brown Fur: Basecoat with Burnt Umber + Teddy Bear Brown. Darken with Burnt Umber + Licorice. Lighten with Teddy Bear Brown, Teddy Bear Tan, and Teddy Bear Tan + Tapioca.
2. Tan Fur: Basecoat with Teddy Bear Tan. Lighten with Teddy Bear Tan + Country Twill. Highlight with Country Twill + Tapioca.

3. Eyes: Paint the outer area of the eyes with Yellow Ochre + Red Light. Paint the inner area of eyes and outlining with Licorice. Highlight with Tapioca.
4. Nose and Mouth: Licorice.

Black Bear:

Refer to Long Hair Plush Fur on Fur Painting Worksheet. Paint fur with a flat and a round pointed brush.

1. Basecoat with Licorice.
2. Layer on strokes of fur with Licorice + Tapioca. Gradually lighten the shade by adding more and more Tapioca to the mix.
3. Eyes, Nose, and Mouth: Paint with Licorice. Highlight with Tapioca.
4. Bow: Paint with Red Light + Tapioca. Darken with Red Light + Alizarin Crimson. Lighten with Red Light + Tapioca.

Tan Bear:

Refer to Bear Painting Worksheet and to Plush Fur on Fur Painting Worksheet. Paint fur with a deerfoot brush.

1. Basecoat with Teddy Bear Tan. Darken with Teddy Bear Brown + Burnt Umber. Lighten with Teddy Bear Tan + Tapioca.
2. Eyes, Nose, and Mouth: Highlight with Tapioca.

4 Finish

1. When dry, apply two coats of matte acrylic sealer. Let dry.
2. Assemble book. ❏

Fur Painting Worksheet
Types of Teddy Bear Fur

Plush — Deerfoot Brush

Step 1
Basecoat with medium value, Teddy Bear Tan.

Step 2
Stipple on medium dark value, Raw Sienna. Blend.

Step 3
Stipple on dark value, Burnt Umber. Blend.

Step 4
Stipple on medium light value, Country Twill. Blend.

Step 5
Stipple on light value, Tapioca. Blend slightly.

Puffy — Comb, Flat, and Liner Brushes

Step 1
Basecoat with Teddy Bear Tan with a flat brush.

Step 2
Add streaks of medium dark value, Raw Sienna, with a comb brush.

Step 3
Add streaks of dark value, Burnt Umber, with a comb brush.

Step 4
Add streaks of medium light value, Country Twill, with a comb brush.

Step 5
Add streaks of light value, Tapioca, with a comb brush. Add a few streaks with a liner brush.

Long Hair Plush — Flat and Round Pointed Brushes

Step 1
Basecoat with medium value, Teddy Bear Tan, with a flat brush.

Step 2
Add wide streaks of medium dark value, Raw Sienna, with a round pointed brush.

Step 3
Add wide streaks of dark value, Burnt Umber, with a round pointed brush.

Step 4
Add streaks of medium light value, Country Twill, with a round pointed brush.

Step 5
Add streaks of light value, Tapioca, with a round pointed brush.

Worn Fur — Flat, Comb, and Liner Brushes

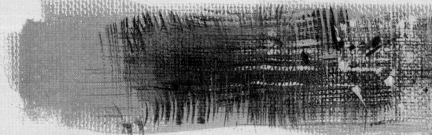

Step 1
Basecoat with medium value, Teddy Bear Tan, with a flat brush.

Step 2
Add streaks of medium dark value, Raw Sienna, with a comb brush.

Step 3
Add streaks of dark value, Burnt Umber, with a comb brush.

Step 4
Add streaks of medium light value, Country Twill, with a comb brush.

Step 5
Add dots and fine lines of all the values with a liner brush.

Bear Painting Worksheet
Painting The Basic Bear

Follow these steps to create a plush, fuzzy bear with dense but short pile fabric. Use a deerfoot brush and a flat brush.

Step 1
Basecoat with Teddy Bear Tan, using a flat brush. Add a darker value paint, Raw Sienna, in the shaded areas. Stipple paint on with a deerfoot brush.

Step 2
Blend basecoat and darker value together by stippling with a dry deerfoot brush. Add darkest value, Burnt Umber, and blend again.

Step 3
Add light values in areas where the light strikes with Country Twill. Blend with a light touch to create the fuzzy fur effect.

Step 4
Add lightest value, Tapioca, in the highlighted areas. Use a very light touch with the deerfoot brush.

Basic Bear

Notice the effect of light shining on the bear. This is created by the use of light, medium, and dark values of paint being placed in the proper arrangement on the bear. The light is coming from the upper left front and shines on those surfaces in line with the light. The absence of light creates dark shaded areas.

Fond Memories

We remember with admiration those talented artists who have passed from life's existence. We remember the beauty they brought to our lives; we remember their patience and caring as they shared their talents and techniques with us; we remember their smiles and the friendship they freely gave.

Diane Capoccia

Diane was innovative and full of energy. She was an excellent painter and enjoyed painting charming child-like characters on wood. Then she discovered the wonderful look she could create by painting on watercolor paper with washes, pen, and ink. Always wanting to stretch and innovate, she started experimenting with embossing of the watercolor paper to create a subtle three-dimensional effect. The look was sensational and was the beginning of an entire product line by Plaid of embossing patterns and tools. Diane always had a new idea to try.

Diane was a friend to new artists. She was always encouraging them and insisting they try publishing their work with Plaid. Brave and outgoing, she was a wonderful model for struggling artists wanting to make a career of sharing their talent. Some of the artists that publish with Plaid today are the result of Diane's nudging. Diane, you left us too soon.

Bette Byrd

Bette Byrd *made* Plaid produce top-quality books. She wouldn't have it any other way. She kindly cajoled and insisted until she got her way. She made us choose the best paper to use in the books; she insisted the books would sell so much better if we used color photography throughout the book (in a time when only covers were color); she wanted bigger books and acclaim for the artists who created the books; and she helped us find the best artists to publish. Bette always sought beauty and excellence. And she made us better for it.

Pictured at right: Bette thought a spiral bound book would make it easier for painters to use the books while they were painting. This book was published in 1977 and was one of Plaid's first full-color painting books.

For more about Bette, see Dedication on page 5.

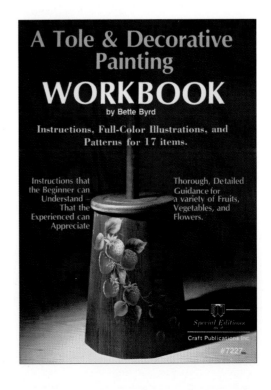

Helen Roberts

Helen taught us how to watercolor in the late 1980's. She was at every national convention of the Society of Decorative Painters sharing her knowledge. Her love of nature spilled over onto us and her warm smile encouraged us as we feebly took brush in hand. She was an excellent and intelligent teacher. She knew her craft and she know how to teach it. Her books were some of our favorites, and were almost textbook-quality in the lessons they contained.

Although Helen was a master watercolorist, she didn't shy away from experimenting with Plaid's new acrylic paint when she was asked. She simply did her homework and adapted her style and technique to using the new Pure Pigment acrylics. Helen was kind, gentle, and talented. We admired her well.

Jacques Zuidema

With a lust for life and a passion to spread his art of old-world folk art to the United States, Jacque stormed into our lives in the mid 80's. That crazy Dutchman painted like a Dutch master. He loved us and we loved him back. But Jacque was merely on loan to us from his home country of Holland. In his country he was renowned and owned the title of the "Dutch National Flower Painter." He was most proud of being chosen from among 200 professionals to paint for Queen Juliana and her husband Prince Bernard. Jacque was not a stay-at-home artist. His painting took him to Saudi Arabia, Japan, Germany, Italy, and America. As Jacque once said, "My wonderful art has taken me many places." Thank you Jacque for coming to our place and expanding our world of art just a bit.